THE THIRD PEACOCK

The Problem of God and Evil

THE THIRD PEACOCK

The Problem of God and Evil

New Revised Edition

Robert Farrar Capon

WINSTON PRESS

By the same author:

Bed and Board
An Offering of Uncles
The Supper of the Lamb
Hunting the Divine Fox
Exit 36
Food for Thought
Party Spirit
A Second Day
Between Noon and Three
The Youngest Day
Capon on Cooking
The Parables of the Kingdom

Cover design: Evans-Smith & Skubic, Inc.

Library of Congress Catalog Card Number: 85-51549

ISBN: 0-86683-497-4

Printed in the United States of America

5   4   3   2   1

Winston Press, Inc.
600 First Avenue North
Minneapolis, Minnesota 55403

To those whom I have taught—
for teaching me most of what I know.

Contents

	Introduction	1
I	Let Me Tell You Why	9
II	Let's Take Stock	19
III	The Heart of the Problem	29
IV	Which Requires a Chapter by Itself . . .	41
V	Time Out	47
VI	Into the Divine Complicity	57
VII	The Hat on the Invisible Man	67
VIII	The Rest of Our Journey	79

Introduction

When *The Third Peacock* was originally published, it began not with a systematic delineation of the "problem of evil" but rather (as you will see in Chapter 1) with a fantasy about the delight of God in the act of creation. My feeling was, and still is, that most attempts at theodicy—at proving that God is good even though the world is full of badness—start off wrong. First, they paint a picture of a very good God indeed: all-wise, all-knowing, all-powerful, all-loving—in fact, the supreme exemplar of just about any virtue you can fasten an *omni-* onto. Next, they produce a grim montage of all the horrors in the world: war, disease, pestilence, cruelty, betrayal, deceit, plus any other evils, natural or moral, they care to include. Then, desperately but gamely, they set about the thankless job of trying to reconcile the beauty of the first picture with the ugliness of the second.

There are two drawbacks to that approach. First, it contains a built-in temptation to get rid of the discrepancy by fudging one of the pictures until it matches the other. Either God has to be toned down into a kind of incompetent who can't be expected to do anything about the mess the world is in, or the mess has to be prettied up until it can be explained away as a blessing in disguise. In neither case, though, is the problem reckoned with, let alone solved; it is simply attenuated into a non-problem.

The second drawback is more fundamental: This "reconciling" approach flies in the face of biblical facts.

Attenuating the problem of evil is, from a scriptural point of view, exactly what God refuses to do. From Genesis to Revelation, he seems instead bent on aggravating it. Unlike the generations of theologians who have been at pains to prove that his public image is not as bad as it seems— who can give you dozens of reasons why the unsavory world he runs is really not his fault— God goes bravely through the entire history of salvation caring not a fig, apparently, for what anyone thinks of him. He is by turns loving and arrogant, bloody and merciful. He promises and does not deliver, he delivers but does not help, he helps in ways that are no help at all—and when he is asked for explanations, he responds only with riddles.

He calls Abraham, for example, and then tells him to kill the only son through whom the call can be fulfilled. He selects Moses and then tries to murder him in an inn. He chooses the people of Israel and then allows them to be flattened, century after century, by every steamrolling superpower in the ancient world. He conquers sin in Jesus' death and then lets sinners go on mucking up the world exactly as before. He overcomes death in Jesus' resurrection and then leaves everybody just as mortal as ever.

But enough. The point is this: If God seems to be in no hurry to make the problem of evil go away, maybe we shouldn't be either. Maybe our compulsion to wash God's hands for him is a service he doesn't appreciate. Maybe—all theodicies and nearly all theologians to the contrary—*evil is where we meet God*. Maybe he isn't bothered by showing up dirty for his dates with creation. Maybe—just maybe—if we ever solved the problem, we'd have talked ourselves out of a lover.

You may object, of course, to such a line of speculation. Indeed, if you're in your right mind, you'd better object to it: It sets standards for the conduct of God's love affair with the world that are lower even than our standards for lunch with an enemy. But you should also understand that your objection has been voiced before —and by experts—to no particular effect on the divine style of loving. The Bible itself is filled with complaints of ill-treatment. From Moses, to Elijah, to the psalmist, to Job, to the Prophets, to Jesus himself, there goes up from its pages, apropos of one bit of divine perfidy or another, a persistent chorus of "How could you *do* this to me?" And yet God neither apologizes nor explains, and he certainly makes no effort to solve the problem of evil for them. He just goes on arranging rendezvous after disreputable rendezvous, no matter how little anyone thinks of his choice of trysting places.

For your comfort, I do realize how unsatisfactory all this must seem: Your thirst for theodicy is being deliberately left unquenched, your itch for understanding not given the benefit of the smallest theological scratch. But just suppose with me for a moment. Suppose that both the thirst and the itch were really for something quite other than intellectual solutions. Suppose that your restlessness for answers were actually—as it was with Job, with Augustine—only the tip of the iceberg, only the upper tenth of a heart's unquietness that could be satisfied by nothing less than the *presence* of this admittedly exasperating God. Ah, then perhaps you see: What a loss it would be to settle for the small beer of theodicy or the short reach of the theological hand. What a shame to palliate the symptoms and leave the deep dis-ease uncured.

This book, therefore, takes a radically different approach to the problem of evil. Instead of asking (on the basis of largely unscriptural theologies), "Why isn't God as good as our intellectual conclusions tell us he should be?" it addresses itself to more manageable, if more uncomfortable questions, namely, "What, in fact, has he actually revealed himself to be like?" and, most important of all, "What do we (not he, please note) propose to do about it?" It strives, in other words, for realism above all else. It takes seriously, not some abstract notion of deity but the kind of deity the God of the Judaeo-Christian Scriptures seems to fancy himself as being—however inconvenient that may turn out to be from a theological point of view. And it suggests in the end that we will be better off accepting the bad manners of a real lover than constructing for ourselves the convenience of a cosmic Lord Fauntleroy Doll.

But lest you think this is either a novel theological approach, or, worse yet, an abandonment of theology altogether, let me give you a longish example from Scripture to prove that such realism has always lain at the heart of genuine theological method.

In the composition of the four Old Testament books of the Kings (commonly referred to in English as 1 Samuel, 2 Samuel, 1 Kings and 2 Kings) a formidable theological mind was at work. The author's object was not simply to present the history of the Chosen People from Samuel, through Saul, through David, through Solomon, through the division of the kingdom, right up to the beginning of the Babylonian Captivity; it was to develop a theological understanding of the relationship between the will of God and all those diverse events and personages. Very early on, therefore, the author of the books of Kings developed a master idea: He decided that the reason the history of God's people went so badly was that their kings regularly and flagrantly transgressed the Law of God.

This theory of historical disaster as God's punishment for leaders' sins went swimmingly for a while. Eli the priest, for example, had disobedient sons; therefore the Philistines defeated the people of Israel. Next, God sent Samuel the prophet to straighten things out, but the people insisted that what they really needed was a king. Neither God nor Samuel thought much of that idea, but eventually they both relented and allowed Saul to become king. Then, however, when Saul disobeyed by failing to destroy the Amelekites utterly, God told Samuel to replace Saul with David. David did fairly well and so passed the kingdom along to Solomon; but Solomon had strange wives who worshipped strange gods and thus, when Solomon died, the kingdom fell apart.

The theory did even better when it came to explaining the terrible history of the divided monarchy: King after king, in the northern as well as the southern kingdom, failed to obey the Law of God. The high places of the pagan cults were not torn down, the laws forbidding intermarriage were not observed, and, in general, every king did what he ought not to have done and left undone what he ought to have done and there was no health in the whole sorry lot of them.

As the theory became more and more attractive, however, so did a corollary implicit in it. Little by little, the theological mastermind behind the books of Kings found himself entertaining ever more enthusiastically the proposition that, if only a king would come along who would really—*really* really—keep the Law . . . well then, everyone would see that both the theory and the corollary were totally accurate descriptions of the way God did business in history. Because *then*, with *that* king, all the disasters would come to a grinding halt and everything would come up roses.

It was at this point that the God of bad manners (especially when it comes to dealing with theologians) decided to throw one of the great sucker pitches of all time. Very near the end of our beloved writer's monumental work (in fact, in the twenty-second chapter of 2 Kings) God serves up to him Josiah, king of Judah—and he drops a sinking curve right across the plate: *Josiah keeps the Law.* Our theologico-historical genius finally has a ball he can hit: Josiah reinstitutes the Deuteronomic Code; Josiah shuts down all the Canaanite high places; Josiah purifies the Temple at Jerusalem and makes it the only center of worship; Josiah keeps the Passover as it had not been kept since the days of the Judges nor during all the days of the kings of Israel or of the kings of Judah. In short, our author receives from God the very king his theories have been itching for over the course of three and four-fifths volumes. And finally, in verse 25 of chapter 23, he takes the swing of his career at it: "Before him was no king like him, who turned to the Lord with all his heart and with all his soul and with all his might . . . nor did any like him arise after him."

And then, guess what? *Josiah dies. In Battle. Slain by Pharaoh Neco of Egypt. Who then takes over Jerusalem, but shortly loses the whole shooting match to Nebuchadnezzar, king of Babylon. Who then leads the Chosen People off into the Great Captivity.* "So much," God says, "for *that* theology. Go back to the drawing board and try again."

To give credit where credit is due, the author of the books of Kings almost did just that. Immediately after his paean to Josiah as the answer to a theologian's prayer, he begins verse 26 of chapter 23 with a word that should probably be given a special name to mark its place in the history of theology. Perhaps we could call it the Great Adversative, or the Grand Nevertheless, or the Ultimate However, or the Quintessential But Still. In any case, and by any translation, there it sits: Tossing his entire theory into the fire of historical fact, he writes (King James Version), "*Notwithstanding*, the Lord turned not from the fierceness of his great wrath"—and with the words turning to ashes in his mouth, he records the details of Josiah's demise.

To be sure, he found himself unable to sustain that kind of theological fact-facing for very long: In the two remaining chapters of his work, he goes back to implying that his theory of divine intervention to punish the disobedient and reward the obedient was still as good as new. But for one gloriously honest moment there, he really did see its falsehood and he paid to the truth the ultimate tribute of that *nevertheless* by which he threw away a lifetime's theologizing.

But even if the author couldn't sustain the honesty, the God who inspired Scripture could, and did. In the writings of Jeremiah during the Captivity and in those of Deutero-Isaiah after it, there are hints that God's relationship to the course of history may be more profound and more paradoxical than the theory of punishment and reward ever imagined. A notion begins ever so slowly to surface: The suffering of Israel may not be simply retribution but the very sign of the mystery of God's own action—of his own involvement—in history. Israel's role as the Servant of the Lord may well be fulfilled more in its failures and defeats than in its successes. And, to carry that notion all the way to what Christians believe is its fulfillment in Jesus, the theological road is open at last to the vision that it is in the midst of our disasters, rather than by deliverance out of them, that God fulfills the promise of his love. In other words, the way is open to the Good News that God in Christ doesn't wait for the world to save itself. Instead of standing at some antiseptic distance from our agonies and our failures, he comes to meet us in the very thick of them: In Jesus, he dies in our death, he becomes sin for our sins, and in the mystery of his resurrection— *without faking a single bit of history*—he invites us to believe that he has made all things new.

I apologize for so long an illustration; but now, perhaps, you see. Christian theologians who address themselves to the problem of evil should treat it as a mystery to be entered, not as a puzzle to be solved. That, accordingly, is just what this book tries to do. At times whimsically, at times earnestly—never solemnly but always seriously—it invites the reader all the way down into the heart of the problem, into the divine complicity in the nightmare at the bottom of the world. If that isn't the way most theologians have dealt with it, it nevertheless remains the way Scripture, considered from start to finish, deals with it. The supreme act by which God makes history come out right—the still, reconciling point of the whole turning world—is the very nightmare of the cross itself. This book simply tries to remove the theological blinders that keep us from seeing—in both our own case and God's—the way things really are.

I am delighted that Winston Press has seen fit to reissue *The Third Peacock* in a new format. While the body of the work remains substantially unchanged, this new edition has provided me with the opportunity to make what I hope are improvements in the text. I'm happy that the book is once again in print, and I wish all its readers Godspeed.

I

Let Me Tell You Why

Let me tell you why God made the world.

One afternoon, before anything was made, God the Father, God the Son and God the Holy Spirit sat around in the unity of their Godhead discussing one of the Father's fixations. From all eternity, it seems, he had had this *thing* about being. He would keep thinking up all kinds of unnecessary things—new ways of being and new kinds of beings to be. And as they talked, God the Son suddenly said, "Really, this is absolutely great stuff. Why don't I go out and mix us up a batch?" And God the Holy Spirit said, "Terrific! I'll help you." So they all pitched in, and after supper that night, the Son and the Holy Spirit put on this tremendous show of being for the Father. It was full of water and light and frogs; pine cones kept dropping all over the place and crazy fish swam around in the wineglasses. There were mushrooms and grapes, horseradishes and tigers— and men and women everywhere to taste them, to juggle them, to join them and to love them. And God the Father looked at the whole wild party and said, "Wonderful! Just what I had in mind! *Tov! Tov! Tov!*" And all God the Son and God the Holy Spirit could think of to say was the same thing. "*Tov! Tov! Tov!*" So they shouted together "*Tov meod!*" and they laughed for ages and ages, saying things like how great it was for beings to be, and how clever of the Father to think of the idea, and how kind of the Son to go to all that trouble putting it together, and how considerate of the Spirit to spend so much time directing and choreographing. And forever and ever they told old jokes, and the Father and the Son drank their wine *in unitate Spiritus Sancti,* and they all threw ripe olives and pickled mushrooms at each other *per omnia saecula saeculorum. Amen.*

It is, I grant you, a crass analogy; but crass analogies are the safest. Everybody knows that God is not three old men throwing olives at each other. Not everyone, I'm afraid, is equally clear that God is not a cosmic force or a principle of being or any other dish of celestial blancmange we might choose to call him. Accordingly, I give you the central truth that creation is the result of a Trinitarian bash, and leave the details of the analogy to sort themselves out as best they can.

One slight elucidation, however. It's very easy, when talking about creation, to conceive of God's part in it as simply getting the ball rolling—as if he were a kind of divine billiard cue, after whose action inexorable laws took over and excused him from further involvement with the balls. But that won't work. This world is *fundamentally* unnecessary. Nothing *has to* be. It needs a creator, not only for its beginning, but for every moment of its being. Accordingly, the Trinitarian bash doesn't really come *before* creation; what actually happens is that all of creation, from start to finish, occurs within the bash: the raucousness of the divine party is simultaneous with the being of everything that ever was or will be. If you like paradoxes, it means that God is the eternal contemporary of all the events and beings in time.

Which is where the refinement in the analogy comes in. What happens is not that the Trinity manufactures the first duck and then the ducks take over the duck business as a kind of cottage industry. It is that every duck, down at the roots of its being, at the level where what is needed is not the ability to fertilize duck eggs, but the moxie to stand outside of nothing—to *be* when there is no necessity of being—every duck, at that level, is a response to the creative act of God. In terms of the analogy, it means that God the Father *thinks up* duck #47307 for the month of May, A.D. 1985, that God the Spirit rushes over to the edge of the formless void and, with unutterable groanings, *broods* duck #47307, and that over his brooding God the Son, the eternal Word, triumphantly *shouts*, "Duck #47307!" And presto! you have a duck. Not one, you will note, tossed off in response to some mindless decree that there may as well be ducks as alligators, but one neatly fielded up in a game of delight by the eternal archetypes of Tinker, Evers and Chance. The world isn't God's surplus inventory of artifacts; it is a whole barrelful of the apples of his eye, constantly juggled, relished and exchanged by the persons of the Trinity. No wonder we love circuses, games and magic. They prove we are in the image of God.

Still though, after you've said that the delight of God is the deepest root of the being of everything, you have to watch that you don't wander off into another error. It's fine to see beta particles, electrons and DNA molecules, guppies, geese, girls and galaxies as responses to immediate divine enjoyment. Just remember that what's sauce for the goose is also sauce for the cancer cell, the liver fluke, the killer whale and the loan shark —that if God is holding all things in being right now, he's got some explaining to do if he hopes to maintain his reputation as the original Good Guy. Or, more accurately (since God steadfastly refuses to show up and explain anything, except by announcing mysteries and paradoxes), *we've* got a lot of explaining to do if we are to go on thinking of him in terms of his reputation.

In short, any talk about creation brings you very quickly to what is called the problem of evil. It should be noted, however, that the problem arises only in certain circumstances. If you can manage to believe in two

Gods, for example—one good and one bad—there is no problem. Evil, in such a system, is as much a part of the show as good.

The same thing would be true if you believed that the world was made by God, not out of nothing, but out of some primeval matter, some *Urstoff* or original glop that God didn't make and that he was simply stuck with. Then you could blame evil on the sleaziness of the raw materials he had to work with and get God off the hook by saying he's doing the best he can.

The problem of evil, in short, exists only for those who believe in God, who believe he made all things out of nothing, and who are stuck with a theology of delight that says that all beings, bar none, exist because he thinks they're just dandy. In other words, it is an invention—in the proper sense: a *discovery*—of the Judaeo-Christian tradition with its God who, right at the beginning of the Bible, keeps muttering Good, Good, Good, at the end of each day's work.

Judaeo-Christian theologians, however, have not always done too well by their discovery. More often than not they have set up the problem of evil in a way that made their attempts at theodicy—at justifying the ways of God to man—seem ridiculous and even cruel. Some of them, for example, solved the problem by saying that God allowed evil in order to teach people useful lessons and make them better persons. You know: He gave us pain so we'd learn to keep our hands out of the fire, disappointments in order to teach us perseverance, unkindness from others to help us grow in charity, and so on. The trouble with that, of course, is the *and so on*: torture, to teach us what? cancer, to improve us how? earthquakes, to advance civilization in what way? the whole bleeding, screaming, dying, lying, cheating, rotting carcass of a once beautiful world to uplift us when?

It simply won't wash. For a few great souls, poverty may be a blessing; for most of us, it is what it is: a curse.

Now and then a terminal disease ennobles; most of the time, it's miles from being even the best of a bad job. To set up God as an instructor who uses such methods is to make him the warden of the worst-run penitentiary of all. The atheist who would rather have no God makes far more sense than the pietist who will take that kind of injustice lying down. The atheist at least sounds like Job; the pietist sounds like hell.

Let's begin, then, by saying that there is ultimately no way of getting God off the hook for evil. By and by I'll make use of a distinction between evil and badness, reserving *evil* for deliberate perversions of being by creatures with free choice, and using *badness* to refer to all the other collisions, contretemps and disasters in the world. Even that distinction, however, helps only slightly. It enables you to blame *voluntary* evil—sin, if you will—on other persons than God; it does not, of course, exculpate God from the responsibility for making free beings in the first place. Sure, my brother-in-law is the one who got drunk and punched me in the nose; but then, why is God so all-fired insistent on preserving my brother-in-law's freedom to gum up everybody's life? Sin is possible only because God puts up with sinners.

The quick retort that I object only to other people's freedom—that I find my own precious and will defend it against all comers—is true enough. It is not, however, an answer to the question of why any of us should be free in the first place. It says only, perhaps, that I am enough of an opportunist to agree with God in my own case—that I like the divine-image business when I profit from it; it sheds no light on the mystery of why he should keep such a shop when he knows it is, at least half the time, a losing proposition.

The last gasp on this line of defense is to say that the fact that he keeps backing such a bad show proves how highly he regards freedom. True enough. And on a good day, when the sun is glistening on the snow, when your bowels are not in revolt and when your brother-in-law has phoned to say he can't make your dinner party, it sounds pretty good. But in the stormy season, in the thick of our own and others' sins, it's only one inconvenient mystery used to cover another.

God is still firmly on the hook. (That he is actually on the hook, of course, is God's own final answer to the whole matter. According to the Gospel, he himself hangs on the cross with the rest of his free creation. If you believe that, it is great comfort; it is not, however, one whit less a mystery.) There is, therefore, even in the fullness of Christian revelation, no untying the knot of freedom. Even in the relatively simple case of moral evil, where you can find somebody besides God to blame for what's wrong at the party, it remains true that things go wrong only because of his stubborn insistence on keeping the party going no matter what. Theodicy is for people with strong stomachs.

Literally. If the case for moral evil is difficult, the case for natural evil—for what I choose to call *badness*—is positively distasteful. There is, of course, no question but that bunny rabbits are lovely. But to allow one's theology of creation to rest content with paeans to all that is cuddly and warm is to ignore precisely half of creation. The rabbit is indeed good, and, in his own mute way, he aggressively affirms his own goodness. The coyote is good too. But when the coyote, in the process of affirming her own goodness, contemplates the delectability of the rabbit, it turns out to be a little hard on the rabbit.

The world of delight that the Trinity holds in being is a rough place. Everything eats everything else, not only to the annoyance of those who get eaten, but to their agony, death and destruction. The rabbit himself does in the lettuce, the lettuce impoverishes the soil, the big fish eat the little fish, the little fish eat the shrimp, the shrimp eat the plankton, the rivers eat the mountains and the sun eats the rivers. And the human race is no exception. Modern children probably think it is: For them, turkeys are not killed and bled; they are mined from freezer cases in supermarkets. In fact, however, humanity has, even at its best, more than a lion's share of the world's blood on its hands. What to say, then, about the goodness of a God who makes a world so full of badness?

Wrong solutions come to mind at once. Paying attention only to what is lovely has already been mentioned: It simply ignores the problem. A more serious error is involved in trying to fob off all the killing and eating on sin—to tie natural badness to moral evil and to say that, if it hadn't been for sin, all the animals would have been vegetarians. That, however, is a bit much. It involves, as someone once observed, the saber-toothed tigers waking up the morning after their creation and wondering why the God who designed them to eat grass gave them so damned inconvenient a set of choppers. Such a gambit never solves the problem of theodicy. It simply arranges to have somebody else's ox gored.

Furthermore, even a vegetarian creation is no answer. It is only our human chauvinism that is satisfied when literal bloodshed is ruled out. The lettuces still, in their own way, take a dim view of having to cease being lettuces; as they can, they fight it. One of the deepest mistakes in theology is to start our discussions of the major activities of creation too high. We act as if only we were free, only we had knowledge, only we were capable of feeling. That's not only false; it's mischievous. It makes us a lonely exception to the tissue of creation, rather than a part of its hierarchy.

Finally, it is not at all apparent, in such a solution, just how sin managed to bring about the general debacle of a bloody creation. It was bloody and destructive long before the only available sinners—human beings—

showed up. To argue that our work was to be the reformer of that destructiveness and that, by sin, we welshed on the job is, of course, possible. It is, however, a bit apocalyptic. It is not easy to see how we, even in our present competency, are able to do much about weaning mackerel away from their fondness for silvers. And to postulate such wonders as our work from the beginning is to revert to the worst kind of prelapsarian aggrandizement of human nature—to return to those strange theologies by which Adam and Eve before the Fall were made entirely of stainless steel and teflon, and knew Greek, Chinese and the periodic table of the elements by heart.

To repeat, it just won't wash. However much we may be able to make out a case for the lion's lying down with the lamb in the eschatological fullness of things, it remains true that no wise lamb thinks much of the idea right now. No, the atheist, once again, is right and the pietist is barking up a tree that never existed. Nature *is* red in tooth and claw. The badness of creation is inseparable from the goodness of creation. It can indeed be argued that moral evil, sin, perversion—the willful twisting of goodness toward nothing—is not necessary to the shape of the world; but there is no way of getting simple badness out of the act. What's good for one thing is bad for another. The human race was no doubt meant to be a kind of referee in the game, to lift it into something higher, wider and handsomer. But that we ever had even an outside chance of abolishing here and now the game of lion eat lamb, crow eat carcass, bugs eat crow, is simply beyond reason.

Whether a solution to the riddle is possible, of course, remains to be seen. Only one thing is clear: There will never be a solution until we stop faking the facts. The world is a very rough place. If it exists because God likes it, the only possible conclusion is that God is inordinately fond of rough places. From earthquakes to earthworms it is all his doing. One or the other of them gets us in the end; here begins, therefore, the consideration.

II

Let's Take Stock

Let's take stock of what we've come up with so far: Evil is assignable to freedom; freedom has to be blamed on God. Now if we're facing facts, that means that God has dangerously odd tastes: He is inordinately fond of risk and roughhouse. Any omnipotent being who makes as much room as he does for back talk and misbehavior strikes us as slightly addled. Why, when you're orchestrating the music of the spheres, run the awful risk of letting some fool with a foghorn into the violin section? Why set up the delicate balance of nature and then let a butcher with heavy thumbs mind the store? It just seems—well, *irresponsible*. If we were God we would be more serious and respectable: no freedom, no risks; just a smooth, obedient show presided over by an omnipotent bank president with a big gold watch.

At least so it seems, until you think about it. Then everything turns around and you're back on God's side before you know it. Try writing a fairy tale on the safe-and-sane view of the universe.

The princess is under a curse. She is asleep and cannot be awakened except by an apple from the tree in the middle of the garden at the Western End of the World. What does the king do? Well, on the theory that a well-run, no-risk operation makes the best of all possible worlds, he gets out his maps, briefs his generals, and sends a couple of well-supplied divisions to the garden to fetch the apple. It is only a matter of getting an odd prescription from an inconveniently located drugstore that doesn't deliver. He uses his power and does the job. The apple is brought to the palace and applied to the princess. She wakes up, eats breakfast, lunch and dinner forever after, and dies in bed at the age of eighty-two.

Everyone knows, of course, that that's not the way the story goes. To begin with, the garden isn't on any of the maps. Only one man in the kingdom, the hundred-year-old Grand Vizier, knows where it is. When he is summoned, however, he asks to be excused. It seems that he's scheduled to die later that evening and therefore cannot make the trip. He happens to have a map, but there's a complication. The map has been drawn with magical ink and will be visible only to the right man for the job. The king, of course, inquires how this man is to be found. Very simply, says the Vizier. He will be recognized by his ability to whistle in double stops and imitate a pair of Baltimore orioles accompanying each other at an interval of a minor third.

Needless to say, the king calls in his nobles, all of whom are excellent musicians. They whistle, sing and chant at the paper, but nothing appears. They serenade it with airs to the lute and with pavans played by consorts of recorders, sackbuts, shawms and rebecs, but still no luck. At last the king, in desperation, tells them to knock off for lunch and come back at two. He goes up on the parapet for a stroll and, lo and behold, what does he hear but somebody walking down the road whistling double stops like a pair of Baltimore orioles!

It is, of course, the Miller's Third Son, local school dropout and political agitator. The king, however, is not one to balk at ideologies when he needs help. He hauls the boy in, gives him the map and packs him off with a bag of Milky Ways and a six-pack of root beer. That night the boy reads the map. It seems pretty straightforward, except for a warning at the bottom in block capitals: AFTER ENTERING THE GARDEN GO STRAIGHT TO THE TREE, PICK THE APPLE AND GET OUT. DO NOT, UNDER ANY CIRCUMSTANCES, ENGAGE IN CONVERSATION WITH THE THIRD PEACOCK ON THE LEFT.

Any child worth his root beer can write the rest of the story for you. The boy goes into the garden and gets as far as the third peacock on the left, who asks him whether he wouldn't like a stein of the local root beer. Before he knows it, he has had three and falls fast asleep. When he wakes up, he's in a pitch-black cave; a light flickers, a voice calls—and from there on all hell breaks loose. The boy follows an invisible guide who's wearing a cocked hat and descends into the bowels of the earth; he rows down rivers of fire in an aluminum dinghy, is imprisoned by the Crown Prince of the Salamanders, is finally rescued by a confused eagle who deposits him at the *Eastern* End of the World, works his way back to the Western End in the dead of winter, gets the apple, brings it home, touches it to the princess' lips, rouses her, reveals himself as the long-lost son of the Eagle King and marries the princess. Then, and only then, do they live happily ever after.

Do you see? It is precisely improbability and risk that make the story. There isn't a child on earth who doesn't know the crucial moment—whose heart, no matter how well it knows the story, doesn't miss a beat every time the boy gets to the third peacock on the left. There is no one still in possession of humanity who doesn't recognize that moment as the sacrament of all the unnecessary risks ever taken by God or man—of the freedom that we cannot live with, and will not live without. True enough, it explains nothing; but it does mark mystery as our oldest, truest home.

Fascinatingly, if you turn from fairy tales to sport or games of chance, you get the same result. What is bridge or poker but the unnecessary pitting of our ability to control against the radically uncontrollable? What is football or baseball but the ritualization of risk? What lies at the root of our fascination with gambling, probability and odds except a deep response of approval to the whole changing and chancy world? And what is love if it's not the indulgence of the ultimate risk of giving one's self to another over whom we have no control? (That's why it does no good to explain freedom by saying that God introduced it to make love possible. The statement happens to be true, but it doesn't illuminate much. The question still remains: Why *love*? Why *risk* at all?) The only comfort is that if God is crazy, he is at least no crazier than we are. His deepest and our best are very close.

The safe universe may be a nice place to visit; but when we're in the market for a home, we don't go to the overstuffed bank presidents with their model worlds. We head straight for the same old disreputable crowd our family has always done business with: the yarn spinners, the drunk poets and the sports who caroused all night in mother's kitchen, and whose singing filled the stairways where we slept.

*   *   *

Admittedly, that is a fey and slightly quixotic justification for freedom. But since it is all you are about to get from me, I propose to move on. Our problem with regard to freedom is not simply that we foolishly object to the risks involved; it is that, even when we accept them, we go right on acting as if the risk extended only to human beings. In our pride, we limit the discussion of freedom to humanity and then have the nerve to wonder why we feel lonely as the only free creatures in a deterministic universe.

The corrective to all of that takes us back to the act of creation and to the question of the precise relationship between God the Creator and all the comings and goings of the universe itself. I've already said that God is not simply the initiator or beginning cause of creation; he is the present, intimate and immediate cause of the being of everything that is. When we say that God is the First Cause, we don't mean the first of all the causes in time. We are not trying to chase him down by going from me, to my father, to my grandfather, and so on, till we stumble upon God making Adam out of dust, or apes, or whatever. We are not going *back* in history but *down* in the present; and we are saying that when you get all through explaining that my fingernail exists because of my body, and my body because of its physicochemical structure, and its structure because of the particles in the atom—that when you have chased down all the intermediate causes that make being *behave* the way it does, you are still going to have to hunt for an ultimate cause that makes being *be* in the first place. You need a first cause to keep all the secondary causes from collapsing back into nothing; and, since they obviously don't collapse, the First Cause must be right in there pitching all the time.

That may or may not appeal to you. Obviously, it is a version of one of St. Thomas' arguments. I don't put it in here, however, to prove the existence of God—only to make sure that you know what I mean when I say First Cause. If the rest bothers you, let it pass; what's already been said is enough to pinpoint the problem.

Look at it. You have God holding everything in being *right now.* You also have the assorted creatures he holds in being eating banana splits, making love, rabbits or plankton, as the case may be, and generally doing what they please and/or can get away with. What is the connection between the act of God that makes them be and their own acts as individual beings?

The answer must be twofold. To be utterly correct, you have to say that the connection is real but mysterious; more about that later. For all practical purposes here, however, it will do quite nicely to say that, by and large, there is no connection. Unless you are an Occasionalist, that is, one who thinks that God is the only actor in the universe and that the whole history of the world is just a puppet show put on by him, then you must grant that it is the rabbits who make rabbits—and for entirely rabbitlike and non-divine reasons.

Consider the stones on the seashore, how they lie. Why is this oval white pebble where it is? Is it here because God himself, in his proper and divine capacity, reached down an almighty hand and nudged it into place? No. God knows where it is, of course, because he is the cause of its being and, in the exchanges of the Trinity, holds it in continual regard. For the same reason, he also knows what it does. But he is not, for all that, the cause of its doing its own thing. The pebble lies in its place because of its own stony style—and because the last wave of the last high tide flipped it two feet east of where it is now, and the right hind leg of my neighbor's dog flipped it two feet west. It is not there because God, either in person or by means of some preprogrammed evolutionary computer tape, has determined that it must be there.

The pebble, in short, lies where it does *freely*. Not, of course, in the sense that it has a mind and will and chooses as we choose, but in the sense that it got there because of the random rattling about of assorted objects with various degrees of freedom. The waves are free to be waves, to be wet and to push. The pebbles are free to sink and to collide and to break. The dog is free to scratch fleas and chase birds. This whole mixed consort then comes together and makes whatever kind of dance it can manage. God may be the cause of its being, but he is, for the most part, only the *spectator* of its actions. He confers upon it the several *styles* of its freedom; it is creation itself, however, that struts its own stuff.

In other words, any realistic view of freedom has to start way below human nature. It has, in fact, to start with the smallest particle of actually existing reality. No matter how restricted anything is—no matter how deaf, dumb and determined it may in fact be—it is at least free to be itself and is therefore, by the creative act of God, free of direct divine control over its behavior.

Needless to say, such a position doesn't sound particularly religious. As a matter of fact, it isn't. Religion is one of the larger roadblocks that God has had to put up with in the process of getting his messages through to the world. The usual religious view is that God has his finger in every pie and, as the infinite meddler, never lets anything act for itself. People bolster such ideas by an appeal to Scripture, pointing out things like the parting of the Red Sea, or Elijah starting fires with wet wood on Mt. Carmel. That won't do, however. To be sure, I am not about to make out a case that God *can't* do miracles—that he can't from time to time stick in his thumb and manufacture a plum if he feels like it. Nor am I going to maintain that he can't answer the prayers of those of his free creatures he has bizarrely said he would take advice from. All I want to insist on here is that most of the time he doesn't meddle; that his ordinary policy is Hands off.

Obviously, it is just that policy that produces the roughness of creation. On November 1, 1755, in the midst of one of the most theologically optimistic centuries in all of history, the great Lisbon earthquake occurred. At that time, most believers had come to hold a theory of the relationship between God and creation that assured them that God took personal care of every contingency and was especially diligent about arranging for the safety and welfare of the elect. Likewise, most unbelievers had nursed themselves to the conclusion that the world was about as perfect a piece of machinery as was possible and would go on functioning smoothly forever.

In either case, the Lisbon earthquake came as a shock; the intellectual tremor was as great as the geological one. How, everyone asked, in a world so well run by God or nature, could such a disaster occur? Why, the theologians wondered, didn't God take care of his elect? What had gone wrong?

The answer, of course, was that nothing had gone wrong—with the universe. What had happened was that the theological theories had been formulated without paying enough attention to the facts of creation. What happened in Lisbon was indeed assignable to God, but not for the reasons people then advanced. Some said it proved there was no God; others hunted for evidence of wickedness sufficient to warrant so fearful a punishment. The trouble with all such attempts to understand was that they went beyond the evidence. First of all, in spite of a few episodes in Scripture where God slapped down sinners, he nowhere promised that he would be a universal moral policeman. Too many scoundrels died in their beds and too many saints went out in agony ever to permit such a notion to be advanced realistically. In fact, when God actually showed up in Jesus, he resolutely refused to judge anyone. Far from being on the side of the police, he ended up being done in by the very forces of righteousness who were supposed to be his official representatives.

Secondly, if God's role in the world was that of a perpetual Mr. Fixit, it had not, to say the least, been particularly self-evident. Once again, consider the facts. When he showed up in Jesus, he did a few miracles. He calmed a storm or two, healed a handful of the sick and fed two crowds by multiplying short rations. If we are being realistic, however, we cannot hold that these things were the announcement of a *program* for the management of creation. They were, of course, signs to identify him as the manager— and they were evidence of the compassionate direction that he intended his management to take. But as a program, they were a flop. Too many uncalmed storms remain, too many unhealed sick, too many hungry and halt. Indeed, when he did his consummate piece of managing, it turned out to be the ultimate act of non-interference: With nails through his hands and feet, he simply died. Whatever else that was, it was the hands-off policy in spades.

No, the Lisbon earthquake was not God's fault for any of the reasons assigned to it by unrealistic theologies. It was God's fault simply because he made the earth the kind of thing it is. If he had made it out of one solid homogeneous block, then it would not have developed a surface condition liable to cracks and shifts. But since he actually made it out of molten slush—and set it to cool, not in an annealing oven, but in frigid space—it was bound to develop a somewhat unstable crust before its center cooled and hardened. Again, if he had not made trees and grass, ducks and geese, sheep and oxen, men and women free to wander about the earth in accordance with the several styles of their freedom, he could no doubt have arranged to have the site of the city of Lisbon unoccupied by anything liable to be injured by earth tremors. Obviously, however, he had no such restrictions in mind. Everything was left, barring miracle, to fend for itself with what freedom it had. It was indeed horrible for so many to die such a dreadful death; it was not at all horrible for the crust of a partly cooled casting to crack a bit under the circumstances.

Once again, we are back to the necessity of facing facts. The world, insofar as we can see, is not stage-managed by God. Neither is it a place in which a few free beings like us fight a lonely battle against vast armies of totally determined creatures like lions, sharks and mountains. It is rather a place in which all things are free within the limits of the style of their own natures—and in which all things are also determined by the way the natures of other things impinge upon them.

It is precisely the free goodness of the Crown Prince of the Salamanders, as he himself conceives it, that makes so much trouble for the Miller's Third Son in the bowels of the earth. It is the marvelous aptitude of aluminum to conduct heat that makes the rowing trip down the river such a trial to the admirable sensitivity of the human backside. There is no badness except by virtue of the goodnesses that compete with each other in the several styles of their freedom. We have not yet, therefore, solved the problem; we have only descended to a deeper level of consideration. The question now is: In a situation so radically and deliberately out of God's control, how does he bring it all around in the end? If he has power—and uses it as he claims—why does it look as if he has none?

III

The Heart of the Problem

The heart of the problem beats strongest in the confrontation between Jesus and the Devil in the wilderness. The account as we have it is condensed and stylized, but the realities are still clear. After Jesus has fasted for forty days and has meditated, presumably, on his coming redemptive work, the Devil makes three suggestions about the best way to get the job done. Christian piety usually hands the Devil the short end of the stick, but it's worth the time it takes to turn the tables and give him his due.

In the first place, the story doesn't cast the Devil simply in the role of the bad guy. On the old Christian theory that the Devil is a real being—a fallen angel, in fact—he couldn't possibly be *all* bad. Insofar as he exists, his *being* is one more response to the creative delight of the Trinity. Being as such is good. There is no *ontological* evil. (*Whether* the Devil actually exists, of course, is a question of fact, the principal evidence for which lies in Scripture. About that, you will have to suit yourself. About the *possibility* of his being, however, you have no choice: He is neither more nor less likely than a duck. A priori objections to his existence are simply narrow-minded.)

Furthermore, the story does not require that we consider all of his *behavior* bad. Perhaps even his motives were good. After all, his suggestions to Jesus are by no means either unkind or unreasonable. What is wrong with suggesting to a hungry man at the end of a long retreat that he make himself a stone sandwich if he has the power to render it digestible? It is perfectly obvious that Jesus ate again sometime, either on the forty-first day or shortly thereafter. He did not acquire his reputation as a glutton and a winebibber by fasting for the next three years.

Likewise, it was not necessarily mischievous to urge Jesus to jump off the Temple and make a spectacular landing. As the Grand Inquisitor pointed out, people need to see some proof of power if they are to believe. They wander through life like donkeys; a good whack with a miraculous two-by-four might be the very thing to get their attention. Even the suggestion that, in return for Jesus' loyalty, the Devil would hand over to him all the kingdoms of the world is not, on the Devil's principles, such a bad idea. It's simply a rather sensible with-my-know-how-and-your-clout-we'd-really-do-some-good kind of offer. After all, God, who was supposed to be running things, wasn't doing a very obvious job of it. Since, in his own view, the Devil was still the Prince of this world—allowed by the divine courtesy to keep his dominion even after his fall—perhaps he could be excused for hoping for a little more cooperation from the Son of God than he ever got from the Father.

In any case, the clincher for the argument that the Devil's ideas weren't all bad comes from Jesus himself. At other times, in other places, and for his own reasons, Jesus does all of the things the Devil suggests. Instead of making lunch out of rocks, he feeds the five thousand miraculously—basically the same trick, but on a grander scale. Instead of jumping off the Temple and not dying, he dies and refuses to stay dead—by any standards, an even better trick. And finally, instead of getting himself bogged down in a two-man presidency with an opposite number he doesn't really understand, he aces out the Devil on the cross and ends up risen, ascended and glorified at the right hand of the Father as King of Kings and Lord of Lords—which is the best trick of all, taken with the last trump.

No, the differences between Jesus and the Devil do not lie in what the Devil suggested, but in the methods he proposed—or, more precisely, in the philosophy of power on which his methods were based. The temptation in the wilderness is a conversation between two people who simply cannot hear each other—a masterpiece of non-communication. If you are really God, the Devil says, do something. Jesus answers, I am really God; therefore I do nothing. The Devil makes what, to him and to us, seem like sensible suggestions. Jesus responds by parroting Scripture verses back at him. The Devil wants power to be used to do good; Jesus insists that power corrupts and defeats the very good it tries to achieve.

It's an exasperating story. Yet, when you look at history, Jesus seems to have the better of the argument. Most, if not all, of the mischief in the world is done in the name of righteousness. The human race adheres devoutly to the belief that one more application of power will bring in the kingdom. One more invasion, one more war, one more escalation, one more jealous fit, one more towering rage—in short, one more twist of whatever arm you have got hold of—will make goodness triumph and peace reign. But it never works. Never with persons, since they are free and can, as persons, only be wooed, not controlled. And never even with things, because they are free, too, in their own way —and they turn and rend us when we least expect. For a long time—since the Fall, in fact—we have been in love with the demonic style of power. For a somewhat shorter time, we have enjoyed, or suffered from, the possession of vast resources of power. Where has it gotten us? To the brink of a choice between nuclear annihilation or drowning in our own indestructible technological garbage.

However we may be tempted, therefore, to fault the divine style of power—however much we may cry out like Job against a God who does not keep hedges around the goodness he delights in—however angry we may be at the agony his forbearance permits, one thing at least is clear. The demonic style of power, the plausible use of force to do good, makes at least as much misery as the divine, if not more. The Devil in the wilderness offers Jesus a shortcut. Jesus calls it a dead end and turns a deaf ear. The great, even well-meaning, challenge to the hands-off policy comes and goes, and God still insists on playing the Invisible Man, on running the world without running it at all. The question is put loud and clear: Why in God's Name won't you show up? And the response comes back as supremely unsatisfying as ever: To show up would be to come in your name, not mine. No show, therefore. And, of course, no answer.

*　*　*

Try another tack.

The difficulty with the policy of noninterference arises not only in redemption—in God's purported action to straighten out a bent creation; it arises just as acutely in what he does to hold creation in being in the first place. He never tips his hand there either.

In spite of the way it is bandied about popularly and even scientifically, the notion of creation is not, and cannot be, a category of physical science. By any ordinary definition, God is not a physical being. Therefore, if all the investigative devices at your disposal rely on the detection of physical phenomena, none of those devices is going to register the presence of God. It doesn't matter whether you are going *back* in time to discover the act by which he initiated the whole process, or *down* in the present to find the hand that makes it be right now; you are never going to find anything except the results of that act, the works of that hand. He may be operating full blast, or out to lunch, or retired, or nonexistent; but physical investigation isn't going to provide you with a single clue as to which is really the case. *Meta*physical investigation, of course, is another matter. A philosophical inference that there is a Creator is perfectly possible; so is a theological assertion to that effect. Both of those disciplines have room for the concept of creation. But in physical science it is only an infrared herring, an invisible quarterback offsides and out of bounds.

While we are at it, this is the place to add a word about the general subject of other hunting expeditions that try to turn up spiritualities in a material world. From time to time, people try to prove the existence of things like the soul, or the mind, or even such ordinary pieces of business as cause and effect, by an appeal to physical science. None of it ever succeeds—and none of it can. There is nothing that happens *in this world*—up to and including the action of God himself in this world—that doesn't happen on some physical basis. There is no love without hands, arms and hearts to give it expression. There are no thoughts unless there are brain cells to make the thinking process possible. There are not even any miracles without physical starting and stopping points. Jesus goes to the wedding feast. Plain water in jugs is succeeded by first-rate wine. Even if he had done the trick with a magic wand, however, there still would have been nothing but wand, jugs, water and wine that was susceptible of material investigation.

That means, if you think it through, that there is nothing here that can't be faked on a physical basis. Since there is no mystical experience without some accompanying physical activity in the brain, it's perfectly possible, if you have the techniques and equipment to produce the proper brain waves, to obtain an effect indistinguishable from true mysticism. We have known that, of course, for a long time: Ether makes philosophers of us all, and so does the newer and more potent panoply of hallucinogens and mind-expanding drugs. But as we become cleverer, we had best be prepared for a vast increase in the power to fake. Since everything a human being does is done physically, our race of geniuses will someday succeed in producing something that can do everything a human being does. What we will not succeed at, however, is finding a physical basis for deciding whether we have made a human being or only a gorgeous troll. For that we will still need a philosopher or a drunk poet—someone, at any rate, who knows the difference between having a blood pump and having a heart.

The technicians, of course, will try to argue us down. In the kind of world we live in, the *reductionist* argument is always possible: Love is only endocrine secretions; thought is nothing but electrical disturbances in brain tissue; miracle is simply a physical incongruity for which we have not yet found a physical explanation. But, by the same token, the reductionist argument is always specious. Anybody who holds that there is more to reality than physical phenomena can rebut it in an instant. Question: How do I know that the whole idea of God isn't just a bunch of electrical impulses in some cells in my head? Answer: How do you know that electrical impulses in brain cells are not God's chosen device for communicating to me the reality of a spiritual nature not otherwise accessible to me? Score? Zero, zero. Time to drop the reductionist argument and get on with the real job.

Apparently there is just no way of getting God to tip his hand. His power as such—even in so direct a use as miracle—remains invisible. The thing to do, therefore, is to stop looking for barefaced manifestations of it. Accordingly, I propose simply to assume his power and then to try and see its relationship to the radical freedom of the things God holds in being. Such a procedure may gall you; you have, perhaps, a congenital aversion to arguments that assume what they set out to prove. In fairness, however, please note that I am not trying to prove anything—only to reach a possible understanding of certain classic assumptions. What I am doing is indeed circular, but it is not argument; this is sightseeing, not proof. If the Devil had spent a little less time throwing dares at the mystery and a little more time just walking around it, he might have discovered what this book is looking for and saved us all a lot of trouble.

What we need, then, is a good instance of an apparent conflict between the fact that things are free and the assertion that God is, at least in some sense, stage-managing history. I suggest, as that instance, the evolution of man—an event that, by all accounts, has been one of the chief battlefields of the conflict. Its circumambulation takes a little time, but it may do some good.

Take first the points of agreement. There is no question, on anybody's theory, but that human beings showed up *at some time* in history. The accepted modern wisdom puts that time very late indeed in the total picture; but even the biblical story has us show up at the end of God's six-day working week. In other words, everyone is agreed that something *happened*, either to the dirt or to the monkeys, to bring about the phenomenon called human nature. Nobody says that we were present from the beginning, or that our appearance needs no explanation.

Second, on the basis of a renewed seriousness about the freedom of the world, the more discerning representatives of both the theistic and the nontheistic sides tend to rule out any determinism about the advent of human beings. For a long time, of course, secular evolutionists talked as if they had a completely deterministic proposition on their hands—as if, in the constitution of matter itself, there was a fully programmed evolutionary scenario. Worse yet, they sometimes even implied that, if only you had enough time and could duplicate the right conditions, you would get the same world all over again. Mercifully, that kind of talk has pretty much ceased. While everyone admits that mutations of fruit flies under laboratory conditions prove the possibility of all sorts of evolutionary leaps, most people concede that such experiments have nothing to say about where, when and how such jumps might take place in a world full of earthquakes, floods and snowstorms. To be sure, when the first little slimy whatsis slithered up on the beach, it must have had evolutionary capacities de luxe. But perhaps it survived its first day only because the sun, which might have fried it to a crisp, was behind the clouds on that particular Tuesday two hundred million years ago.

Theistic thought has improved similarly. The standard nineteenth-century godly response to the menace of evolution was to say that if evolution was indeed the reason why things turned out the way they have, then it achieved that result only because God had previously *involuted* all the developments. Instead of a secular computer tape, they posited a religious one; but with no better result. An electrochemically oriented divine puppet master is still a puppet master; any world run that way doesn't smell even vaguely like the one around us. We have come, therefore, to a more realistic view. Evolution "causes" nothing; it is merely a description of a sequence of results. You might as well say that *history* caused the failure of Napoleon's Russian campaign. It's things that cause things, at whatever opportunities and in whatever styles they can manage. Evolution or History or the Divine Plan or whatever—all of them are, at bottom, *descriptive* and not determinative categories. We have, in short, finally come to the point of being able to see the world—even the world run by God—as a fairly loose show. The fear of the Lord's tightness has been the beginning of at least a little secular wisdom.

At any rate, so much for the agreements. What, against that background, can be said about God's relation to the appearance of man in the world? On the physical side we must, of course, hold out for the freedom of things. On the theological side, however, it seems that we are stuck with a paradox. There doesn't seem to be any way around the necessity of saying that God actually thought up, and arranged for, human evolution. The *mechanics* of the biblical "Let us make man in our image, after our likeness" can be sat loose to; the *theology* of the phrase is inescapable: Man is one of God's own bright ideas. He has got exactly the species he wanted; how in the world did he do it?

Possibility number one: God is adaptable, if nothing else. As the Supreme Realist he takes what he gets. He puts all the stones of creation into an infinite tomato can, shakes them up, dumps them out and says, "Just what I had in mind." He is, in short, a spectator and nothing but a spectator.

Such a view does very nicely by the freedom of things. It will not, however, leave you with anything even halfway like the God who supposedly instigated the Bible. To begin with, miracle is impossible if God is only an infinite Watchbird. Furthermore, if he is simply the passive accepter of all that is, you would expect him to express no opinions or preferences about anything. Needless to say, that is a limitation that the God of the Judaeo-Christian tradition does not seem to have heard about. Try selling Pharaoh the doctrine of Divine Utter Complacence.

What really makes such a view impossible, though, is the theology of delight with which both the Bible and this book began. God actually has *likes;* and nobody, not even God, can have likes without having dislikes. If Adam is the apple of his eye, then anybody (including Adam) who beats up on Adam is bound to end up on the divine s. list. If that's not true, then things are really in rotten shape. If God is merely passive, evolving along with his creation and nodding meaningless approval at everything, that's the worst news of all. We might just manage to put up with an eternal Puppeteer or an omnipotent Tyrant or even an infinite Predestinarian Monster; but to live forever under the sappy smile of an everlasting *klutz* who doesn't give a damn about anything is simply too much.

Possibility number two, therefore: God runs the world by incorporating into the being of everything a *nisus* or tendency toward himself. Man, accordingly, shows up when he does because God always wanted human beings, and therefore built into the natures of prehuman things a drive or thrust toward humanity.

Evaluation? Close, but no cigar.

First, it is a bit short on the freedom of things. A built-in tendency looks suspiciously like the old preprogrammed computer, even if it's posited as part of the very nature of things. It sounds too much like a distinction without a difference—like a verbal and not a real solution of the problem.

Second, while a nisus sounds better than a built-in drive or thrust, it is hard to see how any of them are compatible with the hands-off policy God seems to honor. A pushy God is a pushy God; it doesn't change things simply to hold that his pushiness exerts itself at the roots of being rather than farther up the tree.

Third. At least in the case of the human style of free will, the innate-thrust theory simply contradicts the facts. We are quite capable of making this lovely pinball machine of a world read TILT. There is no subtle nisus that we can't, by the push of a button, or the slow alteration of our genes, play full and final hob with. If God is to be handed a workable device for running creation, it would be a good idea to make it more foolproof than this one. Nisus is nice, but rebellion is more robust. Out with it, then. On to possibility number three . . .

IV

Which Requires
a Chapter by Itself

. . . which requires a chapter by itself to do it justice.

Having thrown out the idea of a nisus because it involved God's doing too much, we are still under the necessity of finding some concept that will not leave him doing too little. There's no use getting rid of a busybody of a God only to find yourself with a substitute who spends eternity drawing unemployment checks.

Accordingly, let me shift the focus of the word *doing*. Most analogies to the creative act of God are unfortunate. Our heads are filled with pictures of responsible little watchmakers and painstakingly careful craftsmen whose products, once brought into being, no longer have any connection with their maker. God's relationship to the world should not be expounded like that. It deserves an analogy that is . . . well, more intimate. What he does to the world, he does *subtly*; his effect on creation is like what a stunning woman does to a man.

In the ordinary sense of the word, she doesn't "do" anything. She needs neither hooks nor ropes nor bumps nor grinds to draw him to her. He doesn't cry out to her, "Don't just stand there; do something." It is her simple standing there that does him in for good. She doesn't touch his freedom, and she doesn't muck about with the constitution of his being by installing some trick nisus that makes Harry love Martha. (Sex, of course, is a nisus, but I'm talking about romance, not sex. If you can't see the difference, you're on the wrong analogical bus.) All she has to do is *be*—and Harry's clock is wound. All in green his love goes riding, and, to the bizarre accompaniment of fleet does, red roebucks, swift sweet deer and four lean hounds, his heart falls dead in the silver dawn.

So God with creation. He makes it, yes. I suppose we shall have to leave him a small shop in the basement of his being where he keeps busy at the day labor of first causing and prime moving. But after that, he doesn't *make* the world; he *makes out* with it. He just stands there, flaunting what he's got and romancing creation around his little finger without moving a muscle.

If, out of mere curiosity, you have to ask *how* he does that trick, I have to admit I have no answer. But then I've never met a man or woman who drew others by love and knew how *they* did it either. The lover is always just as surprised as the beloved. But if you ask in all seriousness how he does it, as if that were a question that needed an answer—then you and I are not only on different buses; we are in different worlds. My answer to you in that case is, "Who cares *how* he turns the world on, as long as he does it—as long as he gets his way by attractiveness, not pushiness." The job of theologians is not to unscrew the inscrutable. Their highest hope is not that their analogical discourse will unveil absolute truth; only that it will make as little trouble as possible. Their criteria are more aesthetic than metaphysical. (I admit that, if pressed to a metaphysical conclusion, I would claim that this particular analogy lies pretty close to the truth. It rests, it seems to me, on a real *analogy in being* between us and God: We turn each other on because we are made in the image of a God who is always on the make. I recognize, of course, that that begs the question; I can't prove my claim. It does have a lovely smell, though. It may be just another circular argument; but the kitchen it prowls around reminds me of the best dinner I ever had.)

Therefore, I'm not averse to playing with the analogy in connection with the first appearance of human beings—or of anything else, for that matter. What is so *attractive* about God that it enables him to draw the world into being? Well, on the basis of the doctrine of the Trinity—in which the Father eternally *thinks up* the world, the Spirit eternally *broods over* the idea and the Son eternally *calls* the world out of nothing into being —maybe it is simply that creation falls, lovely head over round heels, for all that divine fuss over it. Martha moves toward Harry first of all because of the romantic intimation by which she perceives the marvel of his being, leaping upon the mountains, skipping upon the hills, showing himself through the lattice. But she falls hardest at the discovery that he always thinks, broods and says her name: You are beautiful, O my Love, as Tirzah, comely as Jerusalem, terrible as an army with banners. Rise up, my Love, my fair one, and come.

More than that, under his love she *becomes herself*; she blossoms into a fullness of being. *How* she thus evolves is not at all clear; *that* it happens is as plain as day. We talk about her clothes, her hair, her skin, being more *becoming* than they were. We recognize in her a process, not of ceasing to be what she was and becoming some alien thing, but of being called into the fullness of her own being. We see, not a foreign perfection forced upon her from the outside, nor yet some inevitable development deterministically built into her bones; we see a creature in pursuit of her own goodness as pronounced by her lover. He calls her forth, her eyes like doe's eyes, her breasts like twin roes among the lilies and the smell of her garments like the smell of Lebanon —all the things she always could be but never was until they were spoken by him whose name is like ointment poured forth—and she says, Draw me, we will run after you. The king has brought me into his chambers, we will remember your love more than wine.

Admittedly, it is a long fetch from that to a workable application of the analogy to the way God moves the world. Just how the creatures who now lie in the Upper Devonian layer remembered a love more than wine is not obvious; perhaps it will always remain a mystery, sequestered in the mind of Teilhard's "omega point." All we will ever discover, even with great luck, are the mechanisms by which they moved. We will be able to say that the beloved rose up by placing most of her weight on her right leg and using her left arm to steady herself—and that, once up, she ran at a speed of eight miles per hour for a distance of three hundred feet. But the mystery to which she responded remains a mystery still; the ultimate explanation of her whole action is itself inexplicable. Once again, admittedly, no proof. But, once again, the scent of something great.

Do you see? What we really feel the need of when we talk about evolution is precisely the one thing physical science cannot supply: a final reason for it. Its day-to-day devices we may master; but the ultimate desire by which it works escapes us. Oh, I know. Using a word like *desire* for the force that moves the evolutionary process rubs you the wrong way. Nevertheless, I still think it is on the right track. First of all, because it is the only category that can let you have both a free world and a successful God without welshing on either. As I said, I am a theologian—that is, someone concerned to describe creation and God in words that do the least damage to all the facts. Desire, or something like it, is the only idea that does the job.

Just to take the curse off it, though, I should point out that it is neither my idea, nor is it new. It is an old notion that has, unfortunately, been out of fashion since the seventeenth century. As Owen Barfield pointed out, modern physical science has not been an unmixed blessing. Its earthiness, its particularism—its refusal to ask or answer sweeping teleological questions —enabled us finally to pay attention to things in themselves. But it cost us a view of the universe in which things responded to God by love.

When medieval man went out on a starry night and looked up at the heavens, he saw, in one sense, just what you and I see in modern times: innumerable dots of light on a black background. But when he came to explain to himself *what it was* that he saw— that is, when he tried to *understand* what he was looking at, he came up with something very different from our understanding. To us, the heavenly bodies are discreet hunks of matter spinning through space in obedience to assorted laws such as inertia and gravitational attraction. To him, however, the stars and planets moved, not in empty space, but in a vast envelope which he called "mind" or "wisdom"; and they moved, not in obedience to mute physical laws, but by *desire* for the highest good. In other words, to him the planets were part and parcel of a world in which all things interacted and moved in hierarchy. The stars in the sky and the blood in his veins were both participants in a vast, harmonious, and, most important of all, loving universe.

It was just that view of the world that the tidal wave of modern science shattered. Needless to say, it was, in some ways, a view whose hold needed breaking. As long as you thought of blood, for example, as moved by desire within the hierarcy, there was not too much likelihood of your discovering the actual mechanism by which blood circulated within the body. Likewise, as long as you saw the planets moving around the earth in an envelope of wisdom, you were not inclined to raise the question of their actual orbits around the sun.

And yet. For all the benefits the scientific view brought us, it involved a devastating loss. The medieval universe was a friendly, rational, desiring—and desirable—place. The human beings that inhabited that universe felt at home and even important. They were there because of care. The modern universe is not so warm and toasty. It is huge, impersonal and mute. There is no music of the spheres—only silent, mindless laws. We are not at home in it; we are just insignificant pieces of stuff lost in a crowd of vastly bigger but equally insignificant pieces. After four hundred years we cower like skid-row bums on the doorstep of an indifferent creation. We long for a square meal and a kind word, but we're afraid to believe it when we hear it. Mention a universe run by desire for the Highest Good and, for all our loneliness, we can hardly bring ourselves to trust it.

But if we still believe in the real God as he revealed himself—and in the real world as science has displayed it—what else is there? If we're still committed to not going back on either proposition, why not give the old, participative, desiring universe a face lift and put it to work once again? Why not try once more, for all our sophistication, to see the world as the beloved thing whose heart wakes even while it sleeps in the dawn of prehistory? Why not try to hear it rise up at the voice of its Beloved—at the calling of God the Son, who, with the Spirit and for the Father, woos it into being and life? Why not look once again for the Word who *fortiter suaviterque*, mightily and sweetly, orders all things—for creation's Love riding forth all in green and, upon the Virgin's *fiat*, coming down to be Jesu, Joy of Man's Desiring? It's not a case of substituting a mystery for a plausibility; only a matter of letting a lovely mystery take over from a mindless one. If there is even an outside possibility that there really are feet beautiful upon the mountains, what a shame it would be not to run after them!

V

Time Out

Time out at this point, however, for a bite of lunch.

The story of the Miller's Third Son was more apt than it first seemed. I've been leading you, along a path of analogies and concessions, into the doctrine of creation; the journey, however, begins to look more like a slowly winding descent into the bowels of mystery itself. Not only are we getting farther and farther from the daylight of mere intelligibility; we are getting closer all the time to the smell of something dreadful down below in the dark. Somewhere along the line, the third peacock on the left had his way with us. While we still have a little light, therefore, and a halfway decent footing on the concept of a world run by desire, I suggest we sit down on this ledge and ease ourselves.

In the best stories, the standard bill of fare is, I believe, cold venison pie, a good red wine, a couple of apples and some nuts; in any case, that, plus a little conversation, is what I have for you. Of course, if you are one of those sincere types whose conscience makes you eat sandwiches at your desk and work straight through the lunch hour, you had best skip to the next chapter. This theological lolling about in the middle of a quest will make you even more impatient with me than you already are. If, however, you are any kindred spirit at all, have a slice of venison pie and as many pulls on the jug as you like. Theology may be a necessary evil; but there is no excuse for earnestness at noontime.

Venison pie? It's one of the great alfresco delicacies. I have, ever since I put away childish things, made a firm rule: I will eat well-prepared indoor food outdoors, and suitably delicious outdoor food indoors; I will not, however, put myself in the double jeopardy of eating outdoor food outdoors. If I'm to suffer ants, spiders, dirt on my hands and stones under my backside, I must have a touch of civilization to take the curse off it. I'm not so degenerate as to *insist* on the wicker basket and the red-and-white checkered cloth; just degenerate enough to be unalterably convinced that everything tastes better if you have them.

At any rate, venison pie is the archetypal pie that everything else is as easy as. You take a pie plate large enough to accommodate the remainder of your venison stew (which you have made with a good red-wine marinade plus some onions and mushrooms—but without potatoes, dumplings, carrots, parsnips or rutabagas); you line the plate with plain pastry, put in the stew, add a top crust, crimp the edge, cut a *round* hole in the center and bake till the pastry is nicely browned. You then cool it in the tin, wrap it in foil and throw it in your knapsack. With a Cabernet, if you can afford it—or a four-liter jug of red ink, if you can carry it—there is no sickness that destroyeth in the noonday against which you will not have at least a fighting chance. *In vino veritas. Prosit!*

It occurs to me, however, that this may be the first time you have ever had a drink with a dogmatic theologian. If that's the case, let me disabuse you of the prejudices you're more than likely to have. You see, while there have been some of our number who have been "dogmatic" in the pejorative sense of the word, the best of us are the most modest and tolerant people on earth. Contrary to common opinion, dogmaticians are not people who make up their minds first and then tailor the facts to suit their conclusions. They are theologians who accept—on the, to them, likely basis of faith—a number of facts, and who then proceed to tailor their theories accordingly. They are, in a word, the compulsive housekeepers of the Church's intellectual apartment, the maids who modestly sweep up the room after everyone else has done his thing.

Permit me a slightly professional illustration. If you ask liturgical theologians (those gallingly authoritative types who tell you the proper way to worship) what is necessary for a valid celebration of the Lord's Supper, they will inform you that you need, among other things, an invocation of the Holy Spirit, or *epiclesis*. They arrive at that conclusion by observing that all the really dandy Christian liturgies have one. Dogmatic theologians, on the other hand, will tell you that all you need is Christ's words of institution, or something that refers to them. Their conclusion is arrived at, not by judging what makes the best liturgy, but by canvassing all the liturgies that have been considered valid and striking the lowest common denominator. They are concerned, not with achieving the ideal, but with leaving as few invalid Masses as possible lying about in history. They are, in short, not idealogues but broadminded citizens of the particular world they have chosen to inhabit.

And what is true in liturgy is true everywhere else. What dogmaticians say about the Trinity, they say not because *hybris* has led them to think that they know what God is like, but because they are simply trying to keep track of a clutter of assertions about oneness and threeness. Their claim is not that they *understand*, but that they *deliver*; not that you will finally be able to comprehend the contents of the package; only that there will be nothing missing when you get it.

In other words, it's paradox, not intelligibility, that is the hallmark of dogmatic theology. Observe: God is not man, and man is not God; nevertheless, Jesus is both God and man. Those, you will admit, are the assertions of someone who is concerned with more than neatly systematic theories—of a type of mind dedicated to providing you not with answers, but with the raw materials that will enable you to ask the right questions. The best dogmaticians do not argue for the faith; they simply display it and let it fend for itself.

Which leads me to an important distinction. For a long time, apologetics—the art of presenting plausible arguments in favor of the faith—has been considered the absolute queen of theological disciplines. All nonbelievers, and most believers, have lived in the secret fear, or hope, that some hotshot apologist would one day produce the argument that would laugh the enemies of the Lord straight out of court. When you think about it, though, that isn't likely to happen. If the action of God is as mysterious as it seems, it probably isn't going to be susceptible of simple explanations. Waiting around for the light of intelligibility to go on is the guaranteed way to stay in the dark.

Accordingly, it has always seemed to me that the best apologetic of all is dogmatic theology itself: not an attempt at the explanation of things divine, but a hunt for those analogies that will display the beast of the faith in all its oddness. That is why I said that dogmatic theologians' chief tests are always aesthetic, not narrowly rational. They try to come to an appreciation of the given, not to an explanation; to a knowledge, not of what it means, but of how it feels. You can work a lifetime trying to make the Trinity intelligible and get nowhere; you can spend five minutes on it and begin to see its colors light up the world. If I had one piece of advice to bequeath to Christian theologians, it would be: Stick to the dogmatic last. We are, when all is said and done, only preachers of a word we have received. When we stand up on Easter morning and say, "Christ is risen!" we are not arguing for the abstract possibility of resurrection; we are simply announcing what was announced to us. We arrive in our several pulpits not as the bearers of proof, but as the latest runners in a long relay race; not as savants with arguments to take away the doubts of the faithful, but as breathless messengers who have only recently spoken to Peter himself: *The Lord is risen indeed* (gasp, gasp) *and has appeared* (pant, pant, pant) *to Simon!*

Have a little more wine and pass the jug.

The point is that once you master the true method of dogmatic theology, you become the most tolerant of all dispensers of doctrine. Admiration sets you free. Your only real work is to display paradox; after that you can take or leave anything. People rush up to you, for example, and ask for the Christian position on birth control; you find yourself liberated from the necessity of believing that there is a Christian position. Your arsenal of truths consists chiefly of the revealed doctrines of the faith (roughly, the Apostles' and Nicene Creeds—all of whose assertions are quite brief, and fairly factual); after that, all other pronouncements are simply the opinions of assorted Christians. They may run from the *obiter dicta* of Harry in the fifth pew to the encyclicals of John Paul II, but none of them has quite the same stature as the statement that on the third day he rose again. You have, at long last, gotten out of the question-answering business and back into the Gospel-proclaiming business where you belong.

And what a relief that is! Most of the mischief in Christian theology is caused not by answers but by questions. When I was in seminary back in the bad old days, I came across a Roman tract about the Communion fast. It had been reprinted from one of those question-and-answer columns featured by pious magazines. It was signed "Disturbed." I don't remember the answerer's name, but it was undoubtedly something like Paschal O'Flaherty, O.F.M. Cap. "Disturbed" apparently had been lying awake nights wondering about possible sins against the pre-Communion fast as it was then practiced. His question was: May I still receive Communion if, prior to the Mass, I have a nosebleed and swallow some of the blood? Father O'Flaherty responded with a distinction: If the blood proceeds *out* of the nose and into the mouth, the fast is broken and you should not receive; if it proceeds through the back of the nose and down the throat, the fast is not broken and you may receive as usual.

It is almost my favorite illustration of bad theological method. As soon as you tell it to people, they break up. How ridiculous, they say! But think about it. What's wrong with the answer? It makes good sense. Since it is precisely *eating* that breaks the Communion fast—and since all ingestion is not necessarily eating—it makes a perfectly sensible distinction between supralabial and infraglottal ingestion. What is wrong is not the answer but the question. Father O'Flaherty's answer is not foolish; his folly lies in giving any answer at all. A good dogmatic theologian would have said something like "Oh, come now!" and changed the subject.

More pie?

I heard once of a bright young thing who walked out on an inquirers' class and never came back. It seems that an earnest type in the group had asked the priest whether there were any babies in heaven. The reverend gentleman replied, "No, everyone in heaven is thirty-three years old."

Again a case, not of a bad answer but of a dreadful question. If by "thirty-three" you mean what the ancients meant by it—namely, the symbolic age of maturity, the age of Christ in his fullness, the minimum signification of the Latin word *saeculum*—it makes excellent sense: God makes all things perfect in heaven; there will be no half-baked human beings there. If, however, you cannot count on that rather antiquated sophistication in your hearers, you had best recognize the question as a hopelessly high-flying canard and shoot at something more profitable. The only right dogmatic answer to it in this day and age is "I don't know, and neither does anybody else. Let's just say that if God can be trusted to bring heaven off at all, he can be trusted to do it nicely for all concerned."

What dogmatic theologians need above all, you see, is horse sense. Once they admit how little they really know, they can cut the ground out from under almost all their critics. For example, one of the commonest charges against theology is that human language about God is anthropomorphic and therefore, as far as God *in himself* is concerned, meaningless. The idea is that when I say God is loving or good or just or powerful, I'm simply extrapolating human qualities—that my God is nothing more than a hoked-up version of a human being.

The proper dogmatic answer to that is to concede the point. Of course I don't know what God is like *as God*: "No man hath seen God at any time," and all that sort of thing: "My ways are not your ways," saith the Lord. But if there is, in fact, an *analogy in being* between God and man, then human concepts may very well turn out to be analogous to the divine reality. The objector can, of course, reply, "Poppycock! Prove there is such an analogy in being." But the answer to that is "The human race has almost universally assumed it without proof. Darers go first. Prove there isn't one."

When I say that God *knows*, I am obviously using an analogy: I don't understand what the divine knowing is really like; I'm simply grappling for it with the only concept I have. But the same thing is true when I try to describe knowledge that's on a lower level than mine. When I say my dog *knows* something, I may, in my arrogance, presume that I'm expert about all the details of her knowing. But I'm really just as much in the dark about my dog as I am about God. She knows; yes, indeed. There is an analogy in being between her and me, and it works nicely. I spend time—and profitably—training her to know what I mean when I say "Fetch my slippers"; I do not, unless I'm an idiot, spend any time trying to train the ottoman to do likewise. But even when I have trained her to know, do I know *how* she knows? Am I in the least aware of what it is really like for her to *recognize* and *understand* on her own level? I would be an even bigger idiot if I thought I was.

Horse sense. Or dog sense. *All* human language about nonhuman things is anthropomorphic for the simple reason that the only talking animal we have so far discovered is dear old muddleheaded *anthropos*. If our language about God turns out to be invalid, it will be so not because it was human, but because there was no God to talk about. If there actually is a God, however, (and that, obviously, is another question), what we say about him is like what we say about everything else: It's a poking about in the dark by means of analogies. It may be tricky, but it's not necessarily false.

Have an apple.

There are lots of instances of the same thing. People object, for example, to the story of the ascension of Christ into heaven. They trot out all kinds of impressive stuff about how the ancients believed in a three-story universe in which heaven was really straight up. They point out that since we no longer believe in that kind of world—since we know that what's *up* here is really *down* in China—that we have to demythologize the story and get back to the kernel of truth inside the disposable husk of first-century cosmography.

It sounds good, but it isn't even baloney, let alone venison pie. In the first place, no orthodox Catholic or biblical theology requires you to get Jesus farther than the first cloud. After that, you can do what you like. If you think heaven is just another ten thousand feet above his head, go ahead and think it. If you want to be sophisticated and say heaven has no spatio-temporal referent, go ahead and say that. It's an open ball game.

Secondly, the argument tries to have it both ways; it can be run through with its own sword. The objectors are quite willing to give the authors of the ascension story—St. Luke, for instance—credit for *thinking up* a cleverly mythologized account of the basically indescribable mystery of Christ's exaltation. Why aren't they equally willing to give Christ credit for *acting it out*? I'll tell you why. Because they have a prejudice against miracles based, not on modern cosmography, but on nineteenth-century monistic materialism. The horse-sense answer to the whole problem is that if he's God, he can jolly well do what he wants. If he's not God, of course, we're stuck; but, once again, that's another question—and it has nothing to do with the particular brand of celestial mechanics you happen to buy.

You could multiply illustrations all afternoon. Just one more for good measure. People object to the idea that the Bible is the Word of God, just because it is full of oddities, contradictions and dunderheadedness. Admittedly, there have been theologians who tried to maintain that God literally wrote it all himself—or dictated it to infallible secretaries—and that all the riddles of Scripture were put in just to keep our faith on its toes. Well, if you like that theory, you're welcome to it; I happen to think it's rather unflattering to God. What seems more reasonable to me is to assume that God did indeed decide to come up with a bookful of words that would be his Word, but that when he cast about for some word-producing agents, he found that all he had arranged for in his infinite wisdom were human authors. Accordingly, he did whatever he did to inspire the several writers of Scripture and settled for what he got—or, better said, perhaps, he got what he wanted, plus a lot of other sometimes vivid writing that he took as part of the bargain: inflated census figures, rhapsodic reporting of sleazy royal carryings-on, and a fair amount of just plain wrong geography.

My theory about the divine inspiration of 1 Corinthians, for instance, is that God sized up St. Paul on a particular evening and felt that this was the night to get him to tear off the definitive statement about the paradox of the divine power. St. Paul, obedient to the inspiration of the Spirit, promptly responded with chapter one in all its glory: the foolishness of God that was wiser than men, the weakness of God that was stronger than men, and the absolute centrality of the Passion of Christ to the divine management of history. In the process, however, he also produced a rather feeble-minded list of people he thought he remembered baptizing—and followed it up with three chapters full of sexual hang-ups and a couple of pages of absolute waffling on the subject of speaking with tongues. First Corinthians has sixteen chapters not, I think, because St. Paul neatly rounded off his argument at that number, but because God, taking pity on subsequent generations of commentators, inspired him at that point to go to bed.

Be that as it may, however, my own inspiration is to pack up the remains of lunch and get back on the road. It has not, perhaps, been a total loss: Wine is always more pleasantly carried in the stomach than on the back, there is a slice of pie left for later, and you have had the benefit, if it is that, of hearing me explain some of the theological assumptions I have so far foisted on you. In any case, there are still nuts to eat while we walk.

Onward and downward . . .

VI

Into the Divine Complicity

. . . into the divine complicity in the nightmare at the bottom of the world.

We had a brush with it right at the beginning of the book: the fact that there is no possibility, in this kind of world, of getting badness out of the act of creation. If both chicken hawks and chickens proceed from the delight of the Trinity, then God is the author of badness as well as goodness. We woke ourselves up, however, before the worst part of the dream by blaming it all on freedom. We said that freedom was marvelously heady stuff even if it is a pain in the neck.

It wasn't a bad way of shaking off the terror by night the first time around, but it won't work now. Once you've got to the point of seeing the world as run by desire for the overwhelming attractiveness of God— and once you have more than just a pain in the neck to cope with—you want an answer that recognizes the outrageousness of it all, not just an intellectual fast shuffle with a fairy-tale deck. If God draws the world by desire—if the creative Word is really *romancing* into being not only chicken hawks but cancer cells, brain tumors and all the pestilences that walk in the darkness —then he is guilty of something more than a merely laissez-faire attitude toward freedom, of simply tolerating what goes wrong and shrugging it off with an "Oh, things will be things." He is guilty of irresponsible and indiscriminate flattery. He romances the chicken hawk and the chicken at the same time; he sings the praises not only of the beloved child but of the tumor that slowly destroys her sanity. In other words, God is a two-timer; half of his creation is always sitting up nights and crying its eyes out.

Follow that down. As with all two-timers, it's not so hard on the lover as it is on the beloved. God doesn't suffer the consequences. First of all, since he knows everything *eternally*—since both the oldest star and the newest, shortest-lived beta particle have been in his mind as long as he has had a mind—he never has to worry about losing any of the goodnesses he calls into being. Poor little old creatures may not enjoy their participation in the creative bash for very long, but as far as God is concerned the party goes on forever.

Secondly, since he keeps his own participation in his creatures on a strictly spiritual and highfalutin level (God, classically, is neither part of, nor connected with, creation), no thinnest skin ever comes off the divine nose, no matter how many barroom brawls and knife fights creation gets into. He does indeed behold the gore along with the goodness, but it's creation, not God, that feels the crunch. Maybe it even bothers him. But it's still hard to feel very sorry for *him*.

(That, by the way, is what's really wrong with oriental-style religions of indifference—the kind that carry on about God writing straight with crooked lines and using good and bad as if they were just different-colored threads. It's all very well if you're God, or if you're one of those altogether admirable types who can spend a lifetime meditating your way into some nirvana that approximates the divine indifference. But if you're just a common garden slob who cries all night because they have taken away your beloved and you know not where they have laid him, then frankly it looks like a sellout to a con job: the great eternal cat lecturing the mice on the beauties of being eaten, and the mice lining up in the streets to fill the hall. Once again, the only thing that feels right is to cry out against it all like Job: We're your creatures, dammit; we've got *some* rights, haven't we?)

In short, while it's just barely possible, by fabricating an *ersatz* divinity, to tolerate the divine complicity in badness *metaphysically*, it remains unacceptable *aesthetically*. You may philosophize your way into thinking that goodness is worth the risk; but in a world where half of creation is always on the rack, the only thing you can *feel* is that no risk could ever be worth this badness.

Once again, therefore, no answer; and once again, down a little farther.

Our resentment has complex roots. It goes beyond the easily explained distaste that the chicken has for the chicken hawk's advances. Nothing enjoys being killed. After the kill, however, the chicken's own goodness, so recently enjoyed, ceases to be much of a problem for chickendom. True enough, a few chicks may, for a while, retain some sensitive memory of their mother's wings, but even that passes. The situation is tolerable. God has his eternal knowledge of the chicken in all its goodness, and the chickens don't have long enough memories to give them anything but a short-term problem with pain.

It's memory, you see, that puts the sting in our knowledge of badness. God is lucky: He never loses a thing. The chickens are equally lucky: They lose everything. But we are just enough of a mixture of God and chicken to be able to hang on to the worst of both worlds. We haven't got God's divinely intellectual eternal referent of the beloved child before the brain tumor, but we do have a clear memory of a beautiful eight-year-old—a poignant knowledge of what the child's true goodness was really like. Coupled with that, however, we have the actual presence of a deranged child. If we were more divine— or less—it wouldn't be so bad; as it is, it's horrible. It's precisely the remembered goodness that becomes a burr under the saddle of our mind. We run wild intellectually. We lose sight of any possible balance between goodness and badness and call all things meaningless. Things once sweet in our mouth grow bitter in our belly. That we once conversed lovingly with this now alien mind is carrion comfort. The only sane thing we can think of is to curse the day in which we were born and the night in which we were conceived. Why was not sorrow hid from our eyes? Why did the knees prevent us? or why the breasts that we should suck? Only the grave makes sense, where the wicked cease from troubling and the weary are at rest. It is death that we long for, that we dig for more than for hid treasures. Our sighing comes before we eat, our roarings are poured out like the waters. We were not in safety, neither had we rest, neither were we quiet; yet trouble came: the arrows of the Almighty, the poison that drinks up the spirit, the terrors of God. In the end, though, we do grow quiet. Our once glad eye surveys the divine banquet of creation and gives the final withering word: *It has no more taste than the white of an egg.*

No answer, again. But this time we have finally hit bottom.

*   *   *

What shall we say now about the divine complicity?

I've already warned you that I'm not an apologist but a dogmatician—that I'm committed, not to explaining anything, but to hefting it long enough to see what it feels like. For me, therefore, the question is not whether all this can be justified. I suppose it can't be. What I want to get at is the more modest question of whether God has in fact (that is, in his revelation) addressed himself to the problem at all. We may indeed feel like throwing him out of court; nevertheless, if only for the sake of being fairer to him than he is to us, one more look at his announced plan for the management of this losing proposition won't hurt. If it fails to butter his parsnips, so much the worse for him; at least it isn't going to break any more of our bones than already lie scattered before the pit.

The first thing to say is that there's no question but that he has actually promised to make a good show of creation. Quite apart from the subtleties and the paradoxes of the New Testament—which, for all their underhandedness, still end up with the King of Kings riding in on a white charger to make creation his bride without spot or wrinkle—there is the Old Testament, with God himself actually showing up in history every now and then to part a Red Sea or cater a quail dinner.

But what an embarrassment it all turns out to be! Time and again, he fosters the hope of help by the promise of help: "Ask and you shall receive, knock and it shall be opened to you." "The Lord whom you seek shall suddenly come." But he doesn't come dependably enough to keep the hope going. All the advertisements of his help sit squarely against a constant landscape of situations in which no help ever comes—and for which there probably is no help anyway: of battles that the Philistines are bound to win, of impossibilities that even God is not about to convert, and of inexorabilities like death that not even the resurrection of Christ makes a dent in.

If he does help, therefore—if we are to try to believe him in spite of the evidence—how on earth does he do it? Do we have any analogy that might shed light on a divine succour that, as far as anyone can see, makes not one material whit of difference to the creatures he promises to rescue?

Go back a little to the concept of a *desiring* universe, created by the attractiveness of God as God, falling upward like a ton of infatuated bricks for the sheer flattery of the Word. The beauty of that comparison was that it was personal, not mechanical. It saved the freedom of creatures because it allowed us to see God, not as *doing* something—not as meddling, pushing and shoving—but as *being someone fetching.* It gave us, not a divine watchmaker, but a divine lover. Try it again here.

In the Christian scheme of things, the ultimate act by which God runs and rescues creation is the Incarnation. Sent by the Father and conceived by the Spirit, the eternal Word is born of the Virgin Mary and, in the mystery of that indwelling, lives, dies, rises and reigns. Unfortunately, however, we tend to look on the mystery mechanically. We view it as a fairly straight piece of repairwork that became necessary because of sin. Synopsis: The world gets out of whack; perverse and foolish, oft it strays until there is none good, no, not one. Enter therefore God with incarnational tool kit. He fixes up a new Adam in Jesus and then proposes, through the mystery of Baptism, to pick up all the fallen members of the old Adam and graft them into Christ. Real twister of an ending: As a result of sin, humanity ends up higher by redemption that it would have by creation alone.

However venerable that interpretation is, though, it is not the only one. As long ago as the Middle Ages, the Scotist school of Franciscan theologians suggested another. They raised the question of whether the Incarnation would have occurred apart from sin; and they answered yes. In other words, they saw the action of God in Christ, not as an incidental patching of the fabric of creation, but as part of its very texture. For our purposes—in this context of a world run by desire for God —that opens up the possibility that the Word in Jesus was not so much *doing* bits of busy work to jimmy things into line as he was *being* his own fetching self right there in the midst of creation.

And there you have the bridge from a mechanical to a personal analogy to the divine help. When we say that a friend "helped" us, two meanings are possible. In the case where our need was for a Band-Aid, a gallon of gas or a push on a cold morning, we have in mind mechanical help, help for times when help was at least possible. But when nothing can be helped, when the dead are irretrievably dead and the beloved lost for good, what do we mean by telling Martha how much help she was to us in our need? She *did* nothing; she rescued no one from the pit, she brought no one back from the ends of the earth. Still, we are glad of her; we protest that without her we would never have made it. Yet we know perfectly well we could have gotten through it just by breathing in and out. That means, therefore, that what we thank her for is precisely *personal* help. It was her presence, not the things she did, that made the difference.

So with God, perhaps. Might not Incarnation be his response, not to the incidental irregularity of sin, but to the unhelpable presence of badness in creation? Perhaps in a world where, for admittedly inscrutable reasons, *victimization* is the reverse of the coin of being, his help consists in his continuous presence in all victims. At any rate, when he finally does show up in Jesus, that is how it seems to work. His much-heralded coming to put all things to rights ends badly. When the invisible hand that holds the stars finally does its triumphant restoring thing, it does nothing at all but hang there and bleed. That may well be help; but it's not the Band-Aid creation expected on the basis of mechanical analogies. The only way it makes any sense is when it's seen as personal: When we are helpless, there he is. He doesn't start your stalled car for you; he comes and dies with you in the snowbank. You can object that he should have made a world in which cars don't stall; but you can't complain he doesn't stick by his customers.

Nevertheless, being broad-minded, Jesus is blithely paradoxical—or inconsistent, if you like. He reserves the right to start your car for you at such times and places as you and he can work out in conference. Have mercy on me, son of David, says the woman of Canaan; and after a little verbal fencing and a few good *ripostes*, her daughter is made whole from that very hour. It's exasperating. Tidy minds would find him easier to take if he never helped at all. If he's going to make a principle out of victimization, why does he shilly-shally around with occasional answers to prayer?

Once again, it's the mechanical analogy that makes the mischief. Answers to prayers for help are a problem only when you look on God as a divine vending machine programmed to dispense Cokes, Camels, lost keys and freedom from gall-bladder trouble to anyone who has the right coins. With the personal analogy, things are better. The Word is like Martha: Given the circumstances—given the kind of free world he has chosen to make—he will do the best he can by you. It isn't that he has a principle about not starting cars—or about starting them. What he has a principle about is *you*. Like Martha, he loves you; his chief concern is to *be himself for you.*

And since he is God, that is no small item. His presence in the victims of the world—his presence in the cases where even *his* best is none too good—is still the presence of the Word who romances all things into being. Stuck out there in the snowdrift, you may feel he should be doing something more than just trying to make out at a time like this, but he obviously doesn't see it that way. He knows the home truth that grief and love-making are only inches apart. In his own dying, while he hangs helpless on the cross, he still, as the eternal Word, flatters nails into being nails, wood into being wood and flesh into being flesh. Love is as strong as death; there may be waters God does not overcome, but there are no waters that can drown the loving of the Word.

One important refinement, however. People sometimes get the impression that the Incarnation showed up for the first time rather late in the history of the world— that it was not only a patch job, but a patch job after awful and irretrievable damage had been done. Once again, though, it's not as simple as that. There are all kinds of hints that the incarnate Word is not a late intruder, but rather that he is somehow coterminous and contemporaneous with the whole history of creation.

First of all, there is the fact that for God, at least, the Incarnation cannot possibly have been an afterthought. He has no afterthoughts. He didn't one day decide to create and then the next day decide to become incarnate. In his customary eternal style, he always thought of both. Secondly, even the Creed, for all its brevity, suggests that Christ, by "descending into hell," was in some way dealing with those who weren't lucky enough to be born A.D.— that his redemption was somehow available to all of creation right from the start. Finally, there is the witness of the passages that deal with what is usually called the "cosmic" rather than the simply time-bound Christ: Christ the Rock that followed the Israelites in the wilderness; Christ the Lamb slain from the foundation of the world; even Christ the one foreordained *before* the foundation of the world.

His incarnate presence, then, is the presence of the mystery of the Word in all victimization. But, because this is a temporal world—and because in a temporal world, no mystery is ever visible except under a sign— God sacramentalizes the Incarnation. He presents it under a supreme and effective sign in Jesus. The only way to keep track of an invisible man is to put a hat on his head—or in this case, a crown of thorns. Jesus is neither other than, nor a reversal of, what the Word does at all times throughout the fabric of creation. He is the mystery of the Word himself in the flesh. His cross, therefore, is no accident; it is the sacrament of the shared victimization by which he has always drawn all things to himself.

To be sure, in the end of the Gospel he allows himself one success. He rises from the dead. For one morning —and for forty confused days—he takes his hand off the mystery of his working and says, "There! I meant every word I said. The party will come off. Lion and lamb, wolf and kid, will all lie down together. Victimizer and victim will eat at my supper. They shall not hurt nor destroy in all my holy mountains. I will wipe away all tears from their eyes." And then, as the apostles stand dumfounded on the hilltop, he disappears. He claps his hand back over the mystery and says, "But not yet. I have the keys of hell and death, but till the end, I am as good as dead for you. You will meet me in the Passion—in the heart of badness where I have always been. Together, we will make up what remains of my sufferings; in the agony of all victims we will draw the world into the City of God."

From there on, mystery reigns absolutely. It is, I grant you, such an incredible piece of business that no one can be faulted for not believing it. There is no proof, only odd signs that are even more obscure than Jesus himself: a little water, a little bread, a little wine. But if you decide to believe it, what must be done is clear enough: You tend the signs and adore the mystery as best you can; you join your victimization to his; and you say, Jesus, I love you, I love you, till you finally run out of breath.

And then . . .

If it should all happen to be true . . .

VII

The Hat
on the Invisible Man

. . . the hat on the invisible man will have been the very thing that brought us home at last. Or, to update what we used to say back in the days when we were more barefaced about it all: JESUS (as the sacrament of the Word) SAVES; Outside the Church (because it is the sacrament of Jesus) there is no salvation; and even, Ten Thousand Cheers for the Pope! (duly collegialized, of course).

I'm aware that you may have a violent reaction to the turn I've just executed. Some nerve! you say. He quotes Job, knocks God, drags us down to the bottom of the pit —and then has the gall to slip in a plug for organized religion! A fine guide he turned out to be!

By way of a soft answer to your wrath, let me point out that I'm not your guide—or anybody else's, for that matter. I'm simply one of the travelers trapped with you in the bowels of creation. We are all, like the Miller's Third Son, equally in need of a guide. My contribution to our mutual journey has simply been to direct your attention to a peculiar cocked hat bobbing along just ahead of us in the darkness and to suggest that if there is indeed an invisible man under it, he might turn out to be useful—especially if he knows how to get us out of the spot we're in.

For a slightly firmer answer, I have a choice of two different lines of argument. On the one hand, I can deny the charge. "Organized religion" is a misnomer. The Church—anybody's version of it—may look fearsomely organized from the outside, but once you're in it, you have to be deaf, dumb and blind to avoid the conclusion that it's the most disorganized venture ever launched. Its public image may be that of a mighty lion on the prowl; what it really is, in this day and age at least, is a clowder of not too well coordinated pussycats falling all over each other.

On the other hand, I can let your accusation stand and make a useful distinction: The Church is obviously not totally disorganized. At various times in history it has been clever enough to get itself into the teaching business, the building business, the real-estate business, the law-enforcement business, the government business and the witch-hunting business. Its real business, however, was never any of those things. If I'm on the right track, the principal function of the Church is to be the sign of the mystery of the Word— which is precisely what we mean when we call the Church the *mystical* Body of Christ. The principal function of its members, therefore, is the tending of those particular bits of felt and ribbon by which the Church can be recognized as the hat it is supposed to be—specifically, and to be brief about it, the Scriptures and the sacraments.

Obviously, it is not the easiest thing in the world to be content with such a vocation. The Church could, with perfect propriety, be what it once was: a bunch of landless nobodies who met in caves. Its bishops, priests and deacons (whom I take to be essential ribbons on the hat) could be tax collectors, tentmakers and fishermen, and still be the signs of the mystery they were intended to be. Nobody was under any theological necessity to put them on salary or to build them nifty buildings to do their mystical signifying in. Human nature being what it is, however, it was quickly noted that if there was no need for such gussying up, neither was there any theological objection to it. A priest in sneakers saying Mass in a basement is not *more* of a sign of the mystery than a priest in a gold chasuble consecrating the elements in a diamond-encrusted chalice. Accordingly, once it was realized that gold, diamonds and property might go begging, and that pension plans, fringe benefits and annual increments were not necessarily sinful, the Church jumped gleefully into the assorted business opportunities that offered themselves. (It jumped into some sordid ones too, but that's neither here nor there. We're above *that* kind of argument.)

In spite of all such goings on, however, the subject of organized religion has got to come up at this point. If the working of God in both creation and Incarnation is a mystery—that is, if it is always radically invisible—then there is no sense in our getting snootily spiritual about its obvious need for some down-to-earth manifestations. Either God left us to our own guesswork about the spiritualities he was up to, or he didn't. If he didn't, then he had to give us at least a few materialities to provide us with an intellectual handhold. No doubt his originally sparse signs have been multiplied and embroidered; but there doesn't seem to be any way of cooking up a decent version of the Gospel that dispenses with them altogether. If God is doing anything more than just sitting up in heaven and handing out free advice—if he really is *doing* something down here that he intends to let us in on—then, by the necessities of our nature and his, he is forced into sacramentalizing it.

In other words, there can never be a completely spiritual version of the Christian religion. Not that it hasn't been attempted. There have always been itchy souls in the Church who are allergic to materiality. For example, you find Christians who argue that if the deepest reality of the Eucharist is the presence of Jesus himself, then the signs of bread and wine are mere symbols that can be switched around at our pleasure. Beer and pretzels, or crackers and milk, will do just as well.

Their fallacy stems from forgetting that the sacraments are precisely hats on an invisible man. To be sure, if the Word had decided to wear a beer-and-pretzel hat instead of a bread-and-wine hat, he would have been perfectly within his rights: It's his head and his hat. But once he has announced that the bread-and-wine hat is his choice for the late afternoon of the world, we had best keep a careful eye on *that*. It is, after all, the only one under which we *know* he has promised to make himself available.

Needless to say, he's also available and active everywhere else: You can look up the invisible man on the golf course any time you like. That's not the point. The problem on the golf course is that it's hard to be sure you've got hold of the right invisible man—or, indeed, of anything more than one of your own bright ideas. It's not a question of presence; it's a question of how to know when you've grasped it. If I'm right, for example, the mystery that the Eucharist signifies is present throughout creation; the incarnate Word does not become *more present* at the Mass than he is elsewhere. What happens at the consecration is that his presence is sacramentalized for us under a device of his own choosing. We have his assurance for the device of bread and wine; the best you can say about beer and pretzels is maybe—which you could just as well say about ducks, dogs or dandelions.

Once again, the mischief is caused by mechanical analogies. Most of the bad trips in eucharistic theology have been caused by attempting to explain how, in the consecration, God "confects" something new. If we resort to a personal analogy, however, things are less gross. On that basis we assert, not that God *does* something he never did before on land or sea, but rather that he *bees* (forgive the barbarism; English has always needed a more aggressive word than *is*)—that he *bees* what he has always been, but under a special sign.

The sacraments, accordingly, are not mere representations; they are the very realities the Church has always claimed they were: The Holy Communion is Jesus himself, really and effectively; Baptism is the power of God grafting us into Christ; the ordained priesthood is none other than the priesthood of the Word himself. The sacraments, however, do not have an exclusivity in these things. The priesthood the priest bears is not something the layperson lacks: If Baptism gives us the fullness of Christ, there is nothing left for ordination to *add*. Rather, the sacramental priesthood is an effective sign, a notable outcropping, of what the whole Church has. It is every Christian's invisible priesthood packaged and labeled for easy use. Likewise, at the Eucharist, Jesus does not show up in a room from which he was absent. The eucharistic "change," it seems to me, is neither a quantitative nor even, properly, an ontological matter. It's qualitative—a clear but subtle shift in God's style which makes it possible, under the form of an occasional meal, for his creatures effectively to take the Word's constant mystery of victimization and victory into their ordinary exchanges.

It is when you come to Baptism, however, that this line of reasoning bears the best fruit. The Church has always had a problem explaining its relationship to the world. By far the commonest view is the Noah's Ark theory: The human race is out there bobbing around in the drink. Nobody can touch bottom; they all just tread water till they drown. Up over the horizon sails the Ark of Salvation. Much bustle. Cries of "Man overboard!" and "Heave to!" Apostles, Martyrs, Popes, Confessors, Bishops, Virgins and Widows lean over the sides with baptismal boat hooks and haul the willing ones up over the gunwales. Assorted purblind types, however, refuse to come aboard. Sensible arguments are offered to them but there are no takers. After a just interval, the Captain orders full speed ahead and, swamping the finally impenitent in his wake, heads the Church for the ultimate snug harbor.

The trouble with that view, and with many another more refined, is that it forces you to limit the Incarnate Word's saving activity to the Church. No doubt the Church is the only place where you can be sure (by means of easily recognized sacramental hats) that you have a firm grip on what he's doing; but it doesn't seem right to imply that he isn't doing the same work everywhere else. I, if I be lifted up, says Jesus, will draw *all* unto me. *God* invented the ecumenical movement—and his version of it is not limited to Christians. The relationship between the baptized and the unbaptized is not a case of us versus them. The Church is like the rest of the sacraments, an effective sign—a notable outcropping—of what all people already are by the Word's work of creation and Incarnation. The Church is the mystical body because humanity is the mystical body. The only difference is that in church the mystery wears a hat on its head. (Yes, Virginia; that is why a Christian lady always keeps her head covered in church: St. Paul said a hat was power on her head because of the angels. You and I are the first people in history to have figured out what he meant.)

If you would like a little more serious documentation, consider the Christian teaching about the resurrection of the dead. If Christ dwelt and worked only in the baptized, you would expect that the unbaptized would be out of it completely. In fact, however, the promise that the dead will rise is surprisingly indiscriminate. At the Second Coming, *all* are given risen bodies; only *after* the General Resurrection are the lucky sheep separated from the uncooperative goats. Admittedly, you could argue that the entire business applies only to the baptized, but I don't think you can make it stick. It hardly seems consistent either with the divine justice or with the Word's drawing of all to himself, to hand some baptized *schlemiel* a risen body after a lifetime spent as a nogoodnik and then to deny one to a real *mensh* just because he spent his days inside the Warsaw ghetto at the insistence of the baptized. (Don't overinterpret. I'm not saying that anyone is saved apart from Christ. I still buy outright Jesus' statement, "No one comes to the Father but by me." All I'm saying is that the work of Christ is wider than the sacramental manifestations by which it can be grasped. You may, in other words, be able to make it without Baptism; but you'll never make it without the Incarnate Word.)

Even that isn't as bizarre as it sounds. Right from the start, the Church was confronted with the problem of saying something about good converts who unfortunately died before they were baptized. The problem was solved by the invention of the categories of Baptism of Desire (for those who died in their beds) and Baptism of Blood (for those who were helped into the larger life by Nero, Diocletian and Company). It's only a short step from such an accommodation to the wider one I have suggested: Who's to say, since the loveliness of the Word draws all, that desire is possible only to those who have a conscious yen to become Episcopalians or Presbyterians? Who can limit the efficacy of his shared victimization when blood is being shed all over the world? Every year, on December 28, the Church honors as saints all the little Jewish boys whom Herod killed while attempting to put the Incarnate Word out of business. Are we seriously prepared to rule out the possibility that, since the Word is still very much in business, there may be innumerable other innocents who might yet be holy on the same basis?

The upshot of all this is to refocus our attention on the Church's true vocation. Perhaps it's time for it to retire from most of the plausible businesses it has been in for years and to start thinking about its real work as the sacrament of the mystery of the Word. Perhaps it ought to stop justifying its pretension that it is the world's finest question-answering machine and the human race's chief of moral police, and accept the fact that things are a little more obscure and tricky than the Roman Curia, the Episcopalian Mini-Vatican, and the New York Conference of the United Methodist Church have so far seemed willing to admit.

In any case, one thing is certain: There's no point in trying to get all those cantankerous bureaucracies back together under the aegis of a greater bureaucracy still. The only useful thing for the Church to do is join forces with God's already-operative ecumenical movement and learn again how to be a really clear sign of the Passion of the Word. For openers, this means rediscovering the Eucharist as the mirror of its true face; but that's only a start. After that, it probably means a whole new style of life—more care about *being* and less faith in *doing*—and a lot more humility in the process of opening its inevitably bureaucratic but so often unnecessarily flannel mouth.

*　　*　　*

To all of this, two major objections can be raised. The first is that it's unethical—that it's dangerously indifferent to the prescriptive aspect of the Gospel—that it will lead the Church to stop telling people where to head in and so encourage the world to aim straight for the rocks. To which the first response is: Don't kid yourself. Unless you've been asleep since the Middle Ages at

least, you must have noticed that the world lis
Church with somewhat less than eager ears.
rocks; find something better to tell it, or don t waste
your breath.

The second response is more weighty. For the
Church to continue to act as if it were a kind of moral
cop on the beat is to run the risk of perverting the
Gospel. What I have suggested sounds immoral because
God himself sounds immoral. Most of our journey in
this book has been an attempt to get around the divine
complicity in badness; but really, there never was much
chance of success. And when Jesus finally appears as
the ultimate sacrament of the Word, he doesn't help
matters a bit. Parable after parable is deliberately
designed to offend even the most elementary moral
sense: full pay for workers who didn't earn it, and
expensive parties for boys who blew their fathers'
money on booze and broads.

Our trouble is that we've so long let ourselves be
convinced that the Ten Commandments are the whole
story that we're deaf to the outrageousness of the Gospel. The Ten Commandments are only what they are:
ethical prescriptions—and negative ones at that. Even
put positively, they have no more virtue than any other
ethical propositions: They are true comments on the
facts of life, valid expositions of the laws of human
nature. The law of gravity is a useful observation too. It
tells you that if you jump off the Brooklyn Bridge you
will pick up enough speed between the railing and the
river to do yourself a probably fatal mischief. But it
doesn't tell you whether jumping is a good idea or a bad
one. That has to be determined another way: If you
want to end it all, it's not a bad idea; if you want to get
home to dinner, you think less well of it.

Likewise with ethical pronouncements. It's perfectly
correct to say that truthtelling is good for human nature
and that hating is bad for it. The comment is even

slightly useful: If you care about keeping your human nature intact, you will avoid lying and try your best to love. But there are two important questions ethics cannot answer. The first is why you should want to keep yourself in tiptop human shape; and the second is what truths to tell and which people to love. The answer to the first depends on whether or not you think anybody is crazy about you. The answer to the second depends entirely on good taste.

Accordingly, we do both ourselves and the world a disservice when we imply that ethical strictures, if followed, will make all men glad and wise. What they need to hear from us is that the Word loves the world enough to join it in its passion—and that he has exquisitely good taste. They have absolutely no need for a rescue team that stands on the beach and bores suicides with the news that they're drowning. They already knew that; what they really want to hear is some reason why they shouldn't go ahead and sink. Their life tastes like the white of an egg; only a church that knows what it means to be the body of the life-giving Word can possibly be salty enough to interest them.

Which brings us to a second major objection, based on the fear of quietism. To urge the Church to concentrate on *being* the body of the mystery—and to belittle the usefulness of all the more or less plausible things it constantly *does*—is to run the risk of having it do nothing at all. Are we simply to return to the bad old days when, in the blissful assurance of salvation, we told the poor that their poverty was a blessing and justified the deaths of child laborers on the grounds that they were lucky not to have to spend any more time in this vale of tears?

No. The day-to-day actions of the mystical body may not be terribly useful—they may in fact be downright mischievous—but they are absolutely inevitable. The whole mixed bag of clever schemes, bright ideas and gross stupidities is all we have. To be the body of the mystery is to be the body of something you cannot take in hand as such. Accordingly, you take in hand what you can and then relax and trust the mystery to work through you.

Ah, but! you say. That leaves us with nothing more than meaningless busy work.

No again. Precisely because the Church is the body of the creating Word—of the Word who, in the fullness of his delight, romances all things into being—even its minor gestures, even its failures, must spring from a love for what he loves. It does not stay in the slums, work for the abolition of poverty or lobby for civil-rights legislation just because there's nothing better to do. The Church does it because the Word's body must affirm the goodnesses that the Word himself affirms—and if they are threatened, must come to the defense of the victims in whom he suffers. The Church's campaigns are not always successes; there are more helpless cases than not; and, saddest of all, its cures are frequently worse than the diseases it sets out to treat. But it cannot sit idly by. Come down ere my child die, says the world: If Jesus was moved to compassion by that cry, the Church can do no less than second the motion.

It is not passivity that mirrors the Passion of the Word; it is the act of loving in the midst of the desperate helplessness of the world. Quietism is only a parody of victimization; resignation is a door into an empty house. The true Christ does not just stand and wait; he butts his head against the impossibilities until they crucify him; and then, having opened the door of the Passion, he invites the Church into the deepest mystery of all.

VIII

The Rest of Our Journey

The rest of our journey, once we have passed through that door in the bottom of the world, is predictably unpredictable. The Miller's Third Son, following the cocked hat in the gloom, has no idea where he is going or what will happen next. Everyone who reads the story, however, knows that, whatever happens, he will make home safely. Mystery may never stop being mystery; but the happy ending comes on willy-nilly.

It can be argued that the whole business is just an elaborate game of wishing-will-make-it-so. There are answers to that. The first is the old anti-reductionist one-two punch: How do you know that this elaborate game of wishing-will-make-it-so is not the divine device for clueing us in on what, in fact, really is so?

The second is to trot out Pascal's "wager": No matter what happens, we're going to have to wander around down here in the dark of badness as long as we live; why not take a chance on the invisible guide? If he's for real, you win hands down; if not, you only lose what you had to lose anyway. It's a proposition no true gambler would refuse: The worst you can do is break even.

The third answer goes one step further: Even if the invisible guide turns out to be the little man that wasn't there, he sounds nicer than the Crown Prince of the Salamanders. If the whispered love of the Word is a lie, it is at least more appealing than all the ghastly truths we have to put up with.

In the long run, though, who really cares about smart answers? On both sides of the fence, everyone whose head is threaded on straight knows there's no possibility of proving or disproving these things. What we think of them is always decided on the basis of taste. If you find something fetching about the idea of the Word making love to creation in the midst of its passion, you take to it; if not, you call a spade a spade and brand the whole thing a cop-out, a fool's promise to do everything someday by doing nothing now.

But what you *do* about it all is another question. The world commonly assumes that the faithful are uniformly delighted, everywhere and always, by the faith. That's partly because they have never paid proper attention to the Book of Job, and partly because the faithful are sometimes a bunch of fakers who refuse to admit their doubts. There are always days when honest Christians will feel that the promises of the Gospel are just so much incredible baloney. Even when they try to catch the last handhold—the *fact* of the resurrection of Jesus —it gives way and they see it only as the delusion of a handful of peasants, inflated to cosmic proportions by a tentmaker with excess intellectual energy.

But what they *think* has nothing to do with what they *do*.

Ah, you say, intellectual dishonesty!

No. Or yes. It doesn't matter. You forget what kind of proposition we're dealing with. There's no harm in thinking I'm on the wrong bus when, in fact, I'm on the right one—as long as I don't talk myself into getting off the bus. We have been offered a guide who says he can bring us home; either he can, or he can't. But what *I* think about him has nothing to do with *his* competence. I may believe in him with all my heart: if he's a fraud, it gets me nowhere. Or I may doubt him absolutely: if he really knows the way, I can still get home by following him.

You have failed to distinguish between *faith*, which is a decision to act as if you trusted somebody, and confidence, which is what you have if, at any given moment, you feel good about your decision. It's probably not possible to have confidence without faith; but it certainly is possible to act in faith when you haven't a shred of confidence left. Intellectual honesty is a legitimate hint for your own mental housekeeping; it has no effect whatsoever on things that already are what they are.

I suggest, therefore, that we stop this bickering and think about something more pleasant. We still have a long way to go. Have the last piece of venison pie while I tell you a classroom story.

When I teach dogmatic theology, I try to set up the faith on the same framework I've used in this book: the Trinity creating the world out of sheer fun; the Word romancing creation into being and becoming incarnate to bring it home; Jesus as the sacrament of the Word; and the Church as the sacrament of Jesus. Having done that, I then ask the crucial question: How does the story actually end?

Invariably, I get all the correct but dull answers: The Word triumphs; creation is glorified; the peaceable kingdom comes in. And I say, Yes, yes; but how does the story *actually* end? The class looks at me for a while as if I were out of my mind, and then offers some more of the same: The Father's good pleasure is served; humanity is taken up into the exchanges of the Trinity. And I say again, Yes; but how does the story end *in fact*?

No answer. I try another tack: *Where* does the story end? Still no answer. All right, I say, I'll give you a hint: Where can you *read* the end of the story? And eventually someone says: In the Book of Revelation—but who understands that?

I'm not asking you to understand it, I say. I just want to know what you read there. What is the last thing that happens?

And, slowly and painfully, it finally comes out: *The New Jerusalem comes down from heaven to be the Bride of the Lamb.*

They never see it till they fall over it! It's the oldest story on earth: Boy meets girl; boy loses girl; boy gets girl! He marries her and takes her home to Daddy. The Word romances creation till he wins her; *You are beautiful, O my love, as Tirzah, comely as Jerusalem, terrible as an army with banners.* By his eternal flattery, he makes new heavens and a new earth; the once groaning and travailing world becomes Jerusalem, the bride without spot or wrinkle. And finally, as she stands young and lovely before him, he sets her about with jewels, and she begins the banter of an endless love: Jasper, sapphire, a chalcedony, an emerald; *Behold, you are fair, my love.* Sardonyx, sardius, chrysolyte, beryl; *You are fair, my love; you have doves' eyes.* A topaz, a chrysoprasus, a jacinth, an amethyst: *You are fair, my beloved, and pleasant: also our bed is green. Let us get up early to the vineyards; let us see if the vine flourish, whether the tender grape appear, and the pomegranates bud forth: There I will give you my loves. The mandrakes give a smell, and at our gates are all manner of pleasant fruits, new and old, which I have laid up for you, O my beloved.*